Senada Zatagić

A Neglected Right
Prospects for the Protection of the Right to be Elected in Bosnia and Herzegovina

BALKAN POLITICS AND SOCIETY

Edited by Jelena Dzankic and Soeren Keil

1 *Valery Perry (ed.)*
   Extremism and Violent Extremism in Serbia
   21st Century Manifestations of an Historical Challenge
   ISBN 978-3-8382-1260-9

2 *James Riding*
   The Geopolitics of Memory
   A Journey to Bosnia
   ISBN 978-3-8382-1311-8

3 *Ian Bancroft*
   Dragon's Teeth
   Tales from North Kosovo
   ISBN 978-3-8382-1364-4

4 *Viktoria Potapkina*
   Nation Building in Contested States
   Comparative Insights from Kosovo, Transnistria, and Northern Cyprus
   ISBN 978-3-8382-1381-1

5 *Soeren Keil, Bernhard Stahl (eds.)*
   A New Eastern Question? Great Powers and the Post-Yugoslav States
   ISBN 978-3-8382-1375-0

6 *Senada Zatagić*
   A Neglected Right
   Prospects for the Protection of the Right to Be Elected in Bosnia and Herzegovina
   ISBN 978-3-8382-1521-1

7 *Aarif Abraham*
   A Constitution of the People and How to Achieve It
   What Bosnia and Britain Can Learn From Each Other
   ISBN 978-3-8382-1516-7

Senada Zatagić

A NEGLECTED RIGHT
Prospects for the Protection of the Right to be Elected in Bosnia and Herzegovina

Bibliografische Information der Deutschen Nationalbibliothek
Die Deutsche Nationalbibliothek verzeichnet diese Publikation in der Deutschen Nationalbibliografie; detaillierte bibliografische Daten sind im Internet über http://dnb.d-nb.de abrufbar.

Bibliographic information published by the Deutsche Nationalbibliothek
Die Deutsche Nationalbibliothek lists this publication in the Deutsche Nationalbibliografie; detailed bibliographic data are available in the Internet at http://dnb.d-nb.de.

Cover picture: Buliding of Bosnia and Herzegovina parlamentary assembly.
(c) copyright 2019 by Damir Hodžić

ISBN-13: 978-3-8382-1521-1
© *ibidem*-Verlag, Stuttgart 2022
Alle Rechte vorbehalten

Das Werk einschließlich aller seiner Teile ist urheberrechtlich geschützt. Jede Verwertung außerhalb der engen Grenzen des Urheberrechtsgesetzes ist ohne Zustimmung des Verlages unzulässig und strafbar. Dies gilt insbesondere für Vervielfältigungen, Übersetzungen, Mikroverfilmungen und elektronische Speicherformen sowie die Einspeicherung und Verarbeitung in elektronischen Systemen.

All rights reserved. No part of this publication may be reproduced, stored in or introduced into a retrieval system, or transmitted, in any form, or by any means (electronical, mechanical, photocopying, recording or otherwise) without the prior written permission of the publisher. Any person who does any unauthorized act in relation to this publication may be liable to criminal prosecution and civil claims for damages.

Printed in the EU

ABBREVIATIONS

ACHPR/African Commission	African Commission on Human and People's Rights
ACHR	American Convention on Human Rights
ACtHPR	African Court of Human and People's Rights
AfCHPR	African Charter on Human and People's Rights
AU	African Union
BiH	Bosnia and Herzegovina
Dayton Constitution	Annex IV of the Dayton Peace Agreement—Constitution of Bosnia and Herzegovina
DPA	Dayton Peace Agreement
ECHR/the Convention	European Convention on Human Rights
ECtHR/the Court	European Court of Human Rights
EU	European Union
FBiH	Federation of Bosnia and Herzegovina
HRC	The Human Rights Committee
IACHR/American Commission	Inter-American Commission on Human Rights
IACtHR	Inter-American Court of Human Rights
ICCPR	International Covenant on Civil and Political Rights
NGOs	Non-governmental organizations
OAU	Organization of African Unity
OHR	Office of High Representative
PIC	Peace Implementation Council
SAA	Stabilization and Association Agreement
UDHR/Declaration/Universal Declaration	The Universal Declaration of Human Rights
UN	United Nations

TABLES

Table 1	Provisions concerning the right to be elected in the constitutions
Table 2	Prohibition of discrimination in conjunction with the right to be elected in Bosnia and Herzegovina — cases analysis
Table 3	Comparative overview of regional human rights protection of the right to be elected

ACKNOWLEDGEMENTS

This book is based on my Ph.D. thesis defended in October 2019 at the International Relations Department at Selçuk University (Republic of Turkey), where I studied as a Türkiye Bursları scholar. This research is the result of the efforts combining my undergraduate and graduate studies in law and doctoral studies in international relations, and my goal is to emphasize the importance of the right to be elected as well as to contribute to debates on Bosnia and Herzegovina's execution of the European Court of Human Rights rulings and constitutional changes, which has continued for years. I am thankful to my thesis adviser and members of my thesis committee for their support and understanding through this process.

Publishing this book would not be possible without the trust and help of editors at the Ibidem Press—Soeren Keil, Jelena Džankić and Jakob Horstmann—and I am thankful to them for giving me this opportunity and for all the assistance they provided me together with others from Ibidem Press.

I have been lucky to have people around me who have always believed in me and supported me through difficult times—my family members, especially my mother, and Orhan, for always being there for me. This book is for them.

TABLE OF CONTENTS

ABBREVIATIONS 5
TABLES 7
ACKNOWLEDGEMENTS 9

Introduction 13

1. **The Right to be Elected as a Basic Human Right** 29
    1.1. Political Participation 29
    1.2. Active and Passive Suffrage 32
    1.3. Conceptual Development of the Right to be Elected 33
    1.4. Guarantee of the Right to be Elected in International and Regional Human Rights Law 37
    1.5. Guarantee of the Right to be Elected in Comparative Constitutional Law 42
    1.6. Limitations of the Right to be Elected 50

2. **Protection of the Right to be Elected in the European Convention on Human Rights — Case Study of Bosnia and Herzegovina** 55
    2.1. The Protection of the Right to be Elected in Bosnia and Herzegovina 55
    2.2. The European Court of Human Rights' Evaluation of the Cases concerning the Discrimination in Enjoyment of the Right to be Elected in Bosnia and Herzegovina 88
    2.3. The Impact of the European Court of Human Rights Decisions Concerning the Right to be Elected in Bosnia and Herzegovina 111

  2.3.1. The Impacts of the European Court of Human Rights Decisions to the EU-Membership Process..120

3. **Protection of the Right to be Elected in the Americas and Africa** 131
 3.1. Inter-American Court of Human Rights Case Law..131
 3.2. African Court on Human and Peoples' Rights Case Law 139

Concluding Remarks 151
Bibliography..167

Introduction

When Dervo Sejdić and Jakob Finci applied to the European Court of Human Rights (hereinafter: ECtHR or the Court), little did they know it would become an important milestone in both Bosnia and Herzegovina's (BiH) constitutional reform process and human rights protection, in general. This case, and later Azra Zornić and Ilijaz Pilav's cases, raised many questions concerning the discriminative provisions of Bosnia and Herzegovina's constitution. It went beyond by causing serious academic discussions regarding issues of the peace agreements' importance, consociational power-sharing arrangements and the constitutional texts adopted in the peace negotiation processes and the primacy they give to human rights (McCrudden and O'Leary 2013). One important issue, however, was neglected altogether, and that is where this book will focus.

The cases decided by the European Court of Human Rights in 2009, 2014, 2016, 2019 and 2020 concerned racial discrimination in the election process based on ethnic origin. The rights of the citizens of Bosnia and Herzegovina were violated because they did not declare an affiliation with the country's three constituent peoples who make up the majority of the country's population. Those who are Jewish, Roma, Albanian, undeclared of any affiliation, or affiliated but residing in a part of the country where its ethnic group is not a majority are deprived of the right to be elected to the state presidency or second chamber of the parliament in Bosnia and Herzegovina. The Court's rulings confirmed the constitutive provisions prescribing this as discriminatory.

Once the first Court's decision became final, and the process of its execution was about to start, it became clear that its implementation would inevitably have wider consequences for the state's constitutional and political system. The EU intervened in the execution process by setting the implementation of the ECtHR's ruling as a precondition for the negotiation of Bosnia and Herzegovina's membership to postpone dealing with the ruling until a later phase of the country's association process because of the lack of political will. The failure to implement the ECtHR's decisions continued to show up in the EU country progress reports concerning Bosnia and Herzegovina's potential membership, though the EU's authority in the country was undermined (EU 2019).

At the same time, the ruling in the Sejdić and Finci case concerning the country's constitutional system represented the first in which the violation of Article 1 of Protocol No. 12 to the ECHR was declared, drawing international attention, and gaining popularity in academic literature as this protocol introduced general prohibition of discrimination in the European system of human rights protection.

Bosnia and Herzegovina, a country still marred from the war which started in 1992 and ended in 1995 by international intervention, is now governed by a flawed constitution that arose out of the peace agreement — the Dayton Accords. The Dayton Constitution guarantees high human rights standards on the one hand, while protecting interests of the three main ethnic groups in the country on the other, thereby systematically discriminating against minorities and citizens.

Each of the above-mentioned complex issues made the ECtHR rulings in the cases of Sejdić and Finci v. Bosnia and Herzegovina, Zornić v. Bosnia and Herzegovina, Pilav v. Bosnia and Herzegovina, Šlaku v. Bosnia and Herzegovina,

Baralija v. Bosnia and Herzegovina, and Pudarić v. Bosnia and Herzegovina interesting for further investigation. In the initial research phase, I was curious about the ignored legal impacts of these decisions. However, the substantial right violated in all these cases—the right in which the applicants faced discrimination and the right whose protection is so important that it requires constitutional changes in post-war Bosnia and Herzegovina and the Dayton Peace Agreement's overriding power-sharing mechanisms, the right to be elected, deserves greater attention in academic literature. Thus, this book has chosen to focus on this dimension of the ECtHR decisions, with a special emphasis on the protection of the right to be elected both in general and in Bosnia and Herzegovina, specifically.

The existing literature analyzed is mainly composed of political impacts (ESI 2013) and some of the ECtHR decisions' legal impacts (Tran 2011, Claridge 2010). The most significant resource on this topic is Christopher McCrudden and Brendan O'Leary's book *Courts and Consociations — Human Rights versus Power Sharing*, which presents a defense of consociations in favor of a devaluation of human rights' importance. In their book the authors criticize the ruling in the Sejdić and Finci case, questioning the Court's capability to decide on issues concerning states with consociational elements and its overall expertise and objectiveness. Although the ruling in the Sejdić and Finci v. Bosnia and Herzegovina case is analyzed in this book, there is no analysis regarding the protection of the right to be elected, or the ruling's importance or impacts. Rather, the authors defend the idea that the consociational power-sharing arrangements hold greater power and importance than human rights protection simply because they stopped conflict and brought peace in this still divided country.

It is also fascinating that there is little research concerning the prohibition of the discrimination in the context of these decisions. The analyzed decisions were first decided based on Protocol No. 12 to the ECHR, with most of the comments restricted due to the Court's definition of discrimination in this Protocol, which is identical to the definition contained in Article 14 of the ECHR without further analysis in this context as well (Bardutzky 2010).

While there is substantial literature on the impacts from the ECtHR's ruling in the case of Sejdić and Finci v. Bosnia and Herzegovina in matters concerning power-sharing (McCrudden and O'Leary 2013), minority rights and discrimination (Claridge), EU conditionality (Perry 2015, Huszka 2017), and related constitutional essentials of democratic politics (Wheatley 2012) and citizenship (Cirkovic 2014, Džankić 2015), one important area is addressed by the ruling, but relatively ignored by academia: the area of electoral rights, or more precisely, the right to be elected. The Court, while analyzing the applicants' complaints in Sejdić and Finci v. Bosnia and Herzegovina, significantly contributed to the case law concerning Article 3 of Protocol No. 1 to ECHR and interpreted this provision as applicable to the second house of Parliament in cases when its competences concern an important role in the legislative process. This was not commented on in detail in literature. Overall, the substantive right of the issue was merely ignored, and all the attention was directed to the discrimination of minorities' rights, the case's main issue, once more neglecting the right to be elected.

In researching the conceptual framework of this study, I was confounded first by the many synonyms used for passive suffrage and second, by the considerable lack of literature concerning this right. I found only one article (Johns 2016), which stated that there is a gap in literature concerning this concept. In her dissertation, Johns significantly contributes to the conceptualization and justification of the right to be elected as a human right (Johns 2014). Her theoretical justification of the existence of the right to candidacy — the term she prefers — in all liberal democracies is based on the values and interests contained in this right: dignity, autonomy, self-expression, and self-development. The author further argues that the effective exercise of the right to vote and freedom of association, as well as the maintenance of general liberal culture, is not possible without the full enjoyment of the right to be elected. This justification is additionally strengthened through correlative duties of the state which are raised from this right — to respect, to protect, and to fulfill. The philosophical and theoretical framework for the right to candidacy, which Johns establishes in her dissertation, are valuable in arguing for this right's importance.

Another relevant and more recent contribution to the scarce literature on the right to be elected is the edited volume of essays concerning women's rights to be elected in the United States (Piscopo and Shames, 2020), which focuses on this political right's main limitation. Analyzing differences between the right to vote and the right to be elected and examining the guarantees of this right given to women all over the world, Piscopo and Shames argue that the right to vote and the right to be elected need to be accepted as co-equal rights, suggesting that the definition of representational government could change as a result of altering and trusting in democracy. Although narrow and specific, this book contributes to the discussion on the guarantee and protection of the right to be elected, confirming Johns' claim that the right to be elected is an under-researched and under-theorized human right.

After investigating the existing literature on the subject, I concluded that the right to be elected as a human right has often been used interchangeably with similar but inaccurate concepts, or confused with other rights, resulting in its frequent insufficient conceptualization. Moreover, it is often not considered a positive and guaranteed right. Upon this research, I felt motivated to base this book on the right to be elected and its protection. This work's objective is twofold. First, it aims to clarify the conceptual vagueness concerning the right to be elected and its justification as an important human right, which needs to be protected nationally and internationally. Second, it examines and emphasizes this right's growing importance in democratic and democratizing countries.

Analysis of the electoral rights is not possible without contextualizing them within the wider and correlated concepts of democracy and political participation. Each of these concepts is important in defining and understanding the others. There is no democracy without political participation and elections, and electoral rights are the most common way for citizens to exercise their political participation.

Democracy and political participation are wide concepts, often with different meanings attached. The conceptual diversity of democracy includes many other classifications—republican, elitist, deliberative, participatory, electoral, consensus or consociational. Weber, Schumpeter, Popper, Downs, and other theorists have all attempted to describe and analyze democratic processes and politics and define democracy, but the concept's inherent characteristic is exactly its under-determination, which allows development of distinct democratic systems in each country, region, and continent. Perhaps the most concise definition of the concept is evident in Abraham Lincoln's famous Gettysburg Address, in which he described democracy as a "government of the people, by the people, and for the people".

Democracy can change over time, take different forms and pass through different phases in different countries. However, certain elements and principles are accepted as the determinants of democracy such as effective participation, equality in voting, and fundamental rights, to name a few. Democracy guarantees its citizens fundamental rights, ensures a broader range of personal freedoms, helps people protect their own fundamental interests, and provides a maximum opportunity for persons to exercise the freedom to live under laws of their own choosing. Democracies do not fight wars with one another and tend to be more prosperous and developed (Dahl 2015). Furthermore, it is argued that every modern country shall aim to establish "a political system that combines democracy on the one hand with freedom, the rule of law, and good government on the other" (Diamond 2003, 9).

Dissolution of the former Soviet Union significantly increased the number of democratic countries and the varieties between them. Newly independent countries of Eastern and Central Europe initially focused on the institutional aspects of democratic transformation, at the core of which are elections. The Organization for Security and Cooperation in Europe (OSCE) emerged as a leading intergovernmental organization to assist these countries in organizing elections, but also to supervise the election processes to ensure that they would be implemented according to the democratic standards.

The Copenhagen Document contributed greatly to this by requiring states to hold free elections at reasonable intervals through secret ballot and to ensure universal and equal suffrage for adult citizens. It further guaranteed that elected candidates be duly installed in office and allowed to remain in office until their term expires or is terminated, according to legal and democratic procedures (OSCE 1990).

Similar commitments to democracy were numerously repeated at different meetings and events through declarations and resolutions of many international and regional governmental organizations. And while there is no condition or obligation demanding a country to be democratic to qualify as a member of the UN, regional organizations conditioned their memberships by introducing and maintaining democratic government—such as the African Union, the Commonwealth, the European Union, the Organization of American States, and the participating States of the Organization for Security and Co-operation in Europe.

Despite the importance of democracy and its qualities—especially its interconnectedness with human rights—there is no agreement if there is a human right to democracy. The right to democracy was considered an emerging human right already in the beginning of the nineties (Franck 1992), containing an internal aspect of the right of peoples to self-determination and the human rights to freedom of political activity and free and fair elections.

Thirty years later, it is still not an established and guaranteed right. Although some argue that such a right shall be part of customary international law, this is not supported by the main international and regional human rights documents and the interpretation of their relevant provisions. The Universal Declaration of Human Rights, the International Covenant on Civil and Political Rights, and regional human rights documents guarantee rights which can be considered a variation of the right to participation—the right to take part in the government, the right to take part in conduct of public affairs, the right to free elections and to vote and be elected, but not explicitly the right to democracy.

The relevant provisions of these human rights documents use concepts like periodic genuine elections, universal and equal suffrage, secret voting or secret ballot, equivalent free voting procedures, and free expression of the will of electors to explain the guaranteed rights in more detail. All these concepts are embedded in the concept of democracy. Though some of these concepts might intentionally be left vague, others can be interpreted widely. Critics argue that, as conceptualized as they are, these provisions allow for one-party elections and therefore do not guarantee a right to live under democratic government. There is another argument which claims that democracy can be considered a human right because it gives individuals important functions, such as challenging non-democratic regimes and policies before international courts and review bodies, especially concerning restrictions on the political rights of specific individuals, irregularities in democratic processes, structurally undemocratic features of political systems and the absence of democracy altogether (Fahner 2017, 322).

Although these discussions continue, democracy continues to be a widely accepted important goal, ideal and value for states all over the world. The United Nations, European Union and the Council of Europe adopted democracy and democratization as their core values and fundamental principles, which guide these institutions through various projects, programs and initiatives that aim to promote human rights, development, peace, and security, ultimately supporting democracy directly. Strengthening the rule of law, enhancing judiciary and public institutions, fighting corruption, monitoring elections, and empowering the civil sector all contribute further to the development of democracy.

The provisions of international and regional human rights documents guarantee effective participation in government as one of the key features of modern democracies. While the quality of these democracies is measured by the extent and scope of political participation in one country, what is effective participation and how is it evaluated?

Citizens' participation in government can be formal and informal and concerns any citizens activity affecting politics. Although often equated with voting turnout at elections, due to the rise of representative democracies and the struggle for universal suffrage at the beginning of the twentieth century, political participation includes other activities as well: voting, contacting public officials, campaigning, lobbying, being a member in political organizations, running for and holding office, protesting, and volunteering are only some of the most common activities accepted and used to evaluate political participation. Additionally, the last two decades' increased internet usage has made online political activities another form of effective participation. Therefore, while electoral rights may not be the only means of political participation, they may be the most effective and important way of achieving political participation in democracies.

Elections can reflect citizens' influence and therefore play an important role in democracies. Voting is not sufficient, but it is a necessary condition for democracy to exist because without citizens' participation in elections, there is no democracy (Lister and Pia 2015). Through elections individuals have an opportunity to express their political opinion. The importance of electoral rights in every democratic or democratizing country is particularly high. Free, fair, genuine, and periodic elections are one of the pillars of democracy and human rights protections, thus stipulating that there cannot be free elections without full enjoyment of all electoral rights. This interconnectedness is reflected in the provision of Article 3 of Protocol No. 1 to the European Convention of Human Rights, which guarantees free and fair elections. But through the ECtHR's interpretation and its case law, it was accepted that this provision guarantees both the right to vote and the right to be elected.

Electoral rights are political rights, exclusively given to citizens. They include the right to cast a vote (active voting right, universal or active suffrage, (political) franchise) and the right to stand as a candidate (candidacy right or passive voting right). These rights can be enjoyed equally by everyone, without unreasonable or discriminatory restrictions or requirements.

Most of the time, elections are associated with universal or active suffrage, while the related concept of passive suffrage is less known and seldom considered a precondition for determining a level of democratization in a country. On the one hand, this could be a historical legacy, as during the suffrage movement the emphasis was put on voting rights. On the other hand, limiting and restricting candidacy rights is widely accepted as justified. This is still the case as certain groups, such as women and minorities especially, continue to face permitted restrictions in their full enjoyment of the right to be elected.

The striking asymmetry between active and passive suffrage is evident in the conceptual development, legal regulation, and protection of electoral rights. But is there indeed a justification for this, or should electoral rights be co-equal? Clearly, from a human rights aspect, both the right to vote and the right to be elected should be accepted as equally important political rights. The existing literature gap concerning the nature of electoral rights as a human right confirms this hypothesis. It is difficult to find literature concerning the right to be elected, while the right to vote is quite researched and analyzed. All this clearly indicates that the right to be elected is a neglected right, and this needs to be corrected. The right to vote and the right to be elected are co-equal rights, and one without another cannot be fully enjoyed. To fully enjoy the right to vote, a voter must have an opportunity to choose between a wide range of candidates from the ballot list or even to be on the ballot list, if he or she wishes so. Only in these cases is the right to vote fully enjoyed.

The main purpose of this book is to examine the concept of the right to be elected, the guarantees of this right in constitutions, international and regional human rights documents, and the protection of this right under the human rights regimes. The book addresses the existing gaps concerning the right to be elected — conceptual, theoretical, and legal. It aims to contribute to the understanding and importance of the right to be elected as an important human right, establishing a research agenda for future research on this topic. I claim that there is a need to conceptually develop and theorize the right to be elected as a human right to improve its protection in practice.

The theoretical framework of this book is based on institutionalism and regime theory with a special focus on human rights in both international law and international relations. Institutionalism and regime theory are the most suitable international relations theories to explain the human rights regimes and compliance with their rules, as well as the international human rights tribunals and compliance with tribunals' decisions. As a reconciliation theory between liberal and realist traditions in international relations, regime theory explains systems (including human rights regimes) as the reflection of states' interests in which participation is voluntary and a reflection of citizens' interests and preferences.

The right to be elected is established as a human right and guaranteed in many international and regional human rights documents—International Covenant on Civil and Political Rights, European Convention on Human Rights, American Convention on Human Rights (ACHR) and African Charter on Human and Peoples' Rights (AfCHPR). Its protection on an international and regional level, and consequently on the national level as well, depends on states' access and compliance with human rights regimes rules and human rights tribunals decisions. That is why regime theory's importance in analysis and argumentation for better protection of this right is remarkably high.

This book and its analysis employ qualitative methods—document analysis method and case study. Interpretation and systematization of valid law sources, the examination of relevant legal documents (e.g., international agreements, conventions, protocols, constitutions, laws, court decisions), and different acts of political bodies are examples of the document analysis method applied in this book. As a case study, I examine Bosnia and Herzegovina's current constitutional system, specifically its emergence as part of the peace agreement and the function of its controversial provisions, efforts for constitutional changes and the guarantee and the protection of the right to be elected, with the focus on the ECtHR's decision concerning the right to be elected and the process of its implementation.

The first part of the book focuses on the conceptual development of the right to be elected, an essential right for any democratic system, and the guarantees of this important human right. Both active and passive suffrage are important political rights, however, the right to be elected is a lesser known and analysed right. The right to be elected is interconnected with the right to vote, and these rights are mutually dependent on each other. At the same time, both rights are constitutive parts of the universal suffrage and political participation; therefore, the right to be elected is a crucial concept in democratic countries whose enjoyment can only be restricted in exceptional circumstances. Synonyms interchangeably used for this human right significantly impact its conceptual development and clarity in the usage of the concept. Following review of the most essential human rights documents' guarantees and comparative analysis of the constitutional provisions prescribing this right, justifies the importance of the right to be elected at national, regional, and international levels. The concept, scope, guarantee and limitations of the right to be elected in these legal texts are explained and discussed. Finally, the restrictions in ensuring the right to vote and the right to be elected are analyzed and explained in this part of the book.

The second part of the book focuses on the protection of the right to be elected under the European human rights regime and analyzes Bosnia and Herzegovina as a case study in this context. Being the oldest and most successful regional human rights administration, the European human rights regime guarantees protection of the right to be elected for decades. However, while the Court's case law in this area, which is guaranteed under the right to democracy, is underdeveloped, most of its key cases have enabled protection of the right to be elected in Europe. This finds proof in a case study of Bosnia and Herzegovina. The specific character of this post-war state, its constitutional power-sharing arrangements, and their practical impacts, as well as human rights protection are explained and discussed in relation with the cases Sejdić and Finci v. Bosnia and Herzegovina, Zornić v. Bosnia and Herzegovina, Pilav v. Bosnia and Herzegovina, Šlaku v. Bosnia and Herzegovina, Baralija v. Bosnia and Herzegovina, and Pudarić v. Bosnia and Herzegovina. Each of these cases is separately analyzed with the Court's reasons and decisions about the protection of the right to be elected in Bosnia and Herzegovina explained in detail.

The final part of the book provides a comparative analysis of the protection of the right to be elected under the other two regional human rights regimes — American and African. After the detailed analysis of the protection of the right to be elected and case law concerning this right in Europe, this book investigates the guarantee and practical protection of the right to be elected in America and Africa. This book further assesses if and how the right to be elected is guaranteed and protected under the other two regional human rights regimes. Only upon including this assessment in the analysis, it is possible to have a clear idea about the right to be elected.

The primary aim of this book is to raise awareness of an important but neglected human right: the right to be elected. Through investigation of this privilege, this work identifies the existing conceptual and theoretical gap in research in addition to its guarantees and protection under the regional human rights regimes. This book's modest contribution hopes to present a clearer idea of the concept and to raise awareness of the importance of guarantees and better protection of the right to be elected at international, regional, and national levels.

1. The Right to be Elected as a Basic Human Right

1.1. Political Participation

At its core, democracy requires people's participation. No matter the variety of democracy in one country, the rule of the people is an essential element without which there is no democracy. The extent and scope of political participation are important criteria in the assessment of democracy quality as well (Van Deth 2016, 2). However, defining participation is a complex task — there are many ways in which people can participate, and there is no exhaustive list of the types of political participation.

While new ways of political participation emerge, some ways make up the concept of democracy itself. The notion of political participation is often associated with the activities related to elections as result of the rise in representative democracies during the first half of the twentieth century in addition to the suffrage movement. Following these events, the contacts between citizens and elected officials became a common mode of participation, identified as institutionalized or conventional participation. The introduction of non-conventional modes of political participation such as dissent, disapproval, rejection, and provocation followed. At the end of the 1980s and the beginning of the 1990s, political participation evolved into creative participation or individualized collective action, which includes civil activities, volunteering, social engagement, and boycotts. Finally, a connective action term emerged as a mode of political participation that utilizes internet-based technologies.

Briefly, political participation can be defined as "citizen's activities affecting politics" (Ibid). These types of activities, such as casting a vote, signing a petition, or filing an objection to name a few, are voluntary and used by non-professionals or amateurs to address issues concerning governments, politics, or the state. Furthermore, these activities are neither restricted to specific phases nor to specific levels or areas. Political participation can always be defined as active, instrumental, symbolic, voluntary, legal, or illegal behaviors of individuals or groups aiming to express their concerns to the state or its entity (Fox 2014, 500). Even activities such as buying fair-trade products or participating in a suicide protest, behaviors considered nonpolitical but being used for political purposes, can be considered modes of political participation. When several forms of participation share a basic feature, they are called a mode or type of participation. For example, voting and party activities represent an electoral mode of participation.

Elections as a mode of political participation are highly significant. On the one hand, elections enable every citizen's vote to be counted equally, while on the other hand they are considered "the only form of mass political involvement in politics in the modern representative democracies of Europe" (Lister and Pia 2008, 86). Even if this is just a theoretical presumption, elections are the only mode of political participation bearing this characteristic. Despite this, electoral turnout in European democracies is in decline (Ibid, 91).

The situation is not much better in the United States — decreased election turnout is evident and direct results from the change in citizenship norm distribution. These norms concern citizens' duties like reporting crime, sitting on a jury, serving in the military, being active in politics, participating in voluntary groups, etc. Research investigating voter decline reveals that Americans nowadays are less respectful of authority, more distrustful of government and less likely to vote (Dalton 2008, 55). It is presumed that these developments relate directly to the erosion of duty-based citizenship and indirectly to the erosion of electoral participation as well. At the same time, a citizen's repertoire of political participation modes has expanded.

The level of political participation turned out to be directly connected with the country's democratization level — for example, in post-communist countries of Eastern Europe where democratization is relatively new, some modes of political participation are at the lowest level in Europe (Bolzendahl and Coffé). However, arguments exist asserting that this cannot justify undermining the quality of the post-communist democratic process (Kostelka 2014).

As previously stated, democracy and political participation are intricately connected, which is reflected in the human rights dimension of these concepts. The right to democracy could be considered merely a theoretical concept as it is not explicitly guaranteed but derives from global and regional human rights instruments' provisions that occur through the interpretation of norms guaranteeing political participation (UDHR, ICCPR) and free elections (ECHR). And while there are arguments for and against the right to political participation being interpreted as a right to democracy (Cohen 2006, Griffin 2008, Beitz 2009, Peter 2013, Christiano 2011, Fahner 2017), nowadays it is accepted that both democracy and political participation are the existing human rights in theory.

1.2. Active and Passive Suffrage

Active suffrage is a commonly known term of universal suffrage, which means the right to vote. Many human rights documents and national constitutions contain guarantees of universal suffrage, along with descriptions of election process qualities. Passive suffrage, meanwhile, is a lesser-known term, seldom guaranteed in constitutions.

Historically, suffrage movements are one of the most important milestones in the development of human rights. These movements took place in many postcolonial countries at the end of the eighteenth and beginning of the nineteenth centuries. Previously, only wealthy, white men possessed the right to vote, focusing suffrage movements' objectives on securing this political right for everyone, without discrimination based on sex, race, education, or status. It is a common belief that this guarantee has been achieved and that there is almost no country in the world in which the right to vote cannot be enjoyed. However, the reality is that "exclusions from the right to vote remain ubiquitous" (Beckman 2007, 30). Disenfranchisement of children, mentally incapable persons, felons, and non-citizens, to name a few vulnerable groups, is acceptable and considered reasonable. Justification of the exclusion of some people from the right to vote is "ultimately a normative issue that can only be answered by appeal to principles of justice" (Ibid, 42). What was once considered a reasonable excuse for exclusion from suffrage, such as gender, race, or ethnicity, is now neither acceptable nor compatible with the ideas of democracy and a just society.

As this book focuses on the right to be elected, active suffrage will not be analyzed and discussed in more detail herein.

1.3. Conceptual Development of the Right to be Elected

Conceptualizing the right to be elected directly depends on the characterization of this political right as a human right. Without going into detailed explanation and analysis of the nature and importance of human rights, it is sufficient to remark that currently, most human rights are positive rights due to the guarantees mandated by international and regional human rights documents and national constitutions and legislation.

The category of moral human rights, those which are not guaranteed in legal documents but still considered human rights due to their theoretical and philosophical foundations, are not the object of this analysis. This book aims to investigate and identify both the existence of a positive human right to be elected and its protection as such.

Academic literature on the right to be elected is scarce and analyzing and interpreting its existing legal norms in international and regional human rights documents and constitutions will be used to conceptualize the right to be elected as a positive, legal human right.

The preliminary issue in conceptualizing the right to be elected is the range of synonyms used to define it as a political right: the right to stand for elections, the right to stand for office, the right to run for office, the right to candidacy or candidate eligibility, the right to be elected, and the right to be voted for, to name a few. This terminological plurality is further evidenced in the comparative constitutional analysis of relevant provisions which identifies the most commonly used terms as:

- the right to be elected (eleven provisions) — Albania, Ethiopia, Germany, Honduras, Kosovo, Mongolia, Rwanda, Serbia, Somalia, South Sudan, Turkey,
- the right to stand/be (as/a candidate) for election/public office (thirteen provisions) — Angola, Bahrain, Cambodia, Fiji, Gambia, Kenya, Lesotho, Malawi, Marshall Islands, Netherlands, South Africa, Sudan, Zimbabwe,
- the right to run in elections/for office (three provisions) — Egypt, Iraq, Palestine,
- the right to be eligible for elections (two provisions) — Andorra, Congo,
- the right to be qualified for membership (two provisions) — Canada, New Zealand, and
- the right to be voted for in elections (one provision) — Hungary.

The use of many terms for one single concept and one right naturally and frequently leads to confusion academically and politically.

Further conceptual issues occur in the differentiation between being a candidate on a ballot list and being elected and holding an office. These issues call into question which of these guarantees should be contained in passive suffrage or passive voting rights. Some constitutional texts recognize this difference and amend their documents to ensure that both the right to candidacy (different terms are used — stand for public office/elections, being a candidate) and the right to hold office/serving their terms of office or mandates are guaranteed (constitutions of Angola, Fiji, Kenya, South Africa, and Zimbabwe). An individual cannot be elected and hold an office if he or she does not have an opportunity to be a candidate on the ballot list. To be elected, and subsequently hold the office in question, a contender must be a candidate on a ballot list, voted for on election day and win the necessary number of votes. While all these steps are important in the election process, they also represent phases in passive suffrage enjoyment. It is necessary finding the right term to encompass all the stages of this process and leave no ambiguity about the concept.

Most language used for the passive electoral right and listed above are focused on the initial stage of passive suffrage — candidacy. Keeping this in mind begs the questions: what is the situation with guaranteeing and enjoying the latter stages in the process? Are they conditionally or not guaranteed at all? The term "right to candidacy" is arguably not suitable for this right. A right to hold an office (if accepted) as the electoral process' final stage as well as a key stage in passive suffrage might be considered a more suitable term, but it does not exclusively indicate the election process and passive suffrage. So, however conceptually opposed it might be, I find the right to be elected the most suitable term for passive suffrage.

Finally, in theory and literature, broader concepts like suffrage or (political) franchise, political participation, electoral rights and right to democracy are often used instead of the right to be elected, additionally contributing to unclarity concerning the existence and nature of this right. The need to conceptualize and research the right to be elected is further ignored, and the ensuing use of wider, ill-defined concepts continues.

This might not be intentional, but it comes with a price: there is an impression that democracy gives people the right to vote and the right to elect someone to represent them, but not necessarily the right for everyone to be elected. This indirectly limits voters' choices and puts into question the enjoyment of the right to vote as well. Every unnecessary additional limitation in the enjoyment of the right to be elected leads to ballot list intervention and limits of the right to vote.

Both the right to vote and the right to be elected are electoral rights, interdependent and coexistent — one without another cannot be fully enjoyed. This relationship is reflected in two dimensions: 1) the voter's interest to freely choose his representative and 2) the voter's desire to make an informed choice. The first dimension implies multiple options and a qualitative difference between candidates. Without such, elections lose their meaning, as seen in communist systems when election ballots contain only one candidate. While every voter may not always find a suitable candidate or party they wish to vote for, it is important that they have options amongst a "diverse field of candidates which represent wide and varied cross-sections of society" (Johns 2016, 50).

This voters' right can further be seen as a dimension of the right to free expression, as this right concerns the interests of its audience in hearing what is being said. To guarantee the protection of these interests, the right to be elected is conceptualized as an absolute right, limited by the state only in certain justified cases and without procedural restrictions that would unduly disable the realization of the right. This relationship reflects the importance of the right to be elected as it preserves all other human rights, contributing to a common liberal culture.

The right to be elected is nowadays not an absolute right and can be subject to certain restrictions by the states, as the right to be elected is "of obvious importance to the coherence and the development of the democratic state" (Schyff 2005, 363). Therefore, if the right to vote is an implication of a voter's choice, then the right to be elected is an attempt to enable that choice's practical implementation. The interdependence between democracy and electoral rights (right to vote and right to be elected), and the context in which this right exists, are key features in a (liberal) democracy because "its substantive features provide the minimum conditions necessary for the protection of the strong right to candidacy" (Johns 2016, 36).

1.4. Guarantee of the Right to be Elected in International and Regional Human Rights Law

In addition to the literature gap concerning the research of the right to be elected, there is also an evident legal gap concerning this right. On the one hand, some of the most important international human rights documents do not explicitly mandate this political right, but rather, only prescribe a wider right to participate in government. On the other hand, this right's general acceptance guarantees it as a human right on a global and regional level.

One of the legal documents which does not explicitly guarantee the right to be elected is the Universal Declaration on Human Rights (UDHR). While this right is not listed in the Declaration, the right to take part in the government, directly or through freely chosen representatives, is prescribed in Article 21 of the Universal Declaration. This provision provides:

> (1) Everyone has the right to take part in the government of his country, directly or through freely chosen representatives.
> (2) Everyone has the right to equal access to public service in his country.

> (3) The will of the people shall be the basis of the authority of government; this will shall be expressed in periodic and genuine elections which shall be by universal and equal suffrage and shall be held by secret vote or by equivalent free voting procedures.

The International Covenant on Civil and Political Rights (ICCPR), however, does definitively mention the right to be elected in its Article 25:

> Every citizen shall have the right and the opportunity, without any of the distinctions mentioned in article 2 and without unreasonable restrictions:
> (a) To take part in the conduct of public affairs, directly or through freely chosen representatives;
> (b) To vote and to be elected at genuine periodic elections which shall be by universal and equal suffrage and shall be held by secret ballot, guaranteeing the free expression of the will of the electors;
> (c) To have access, on general terms of equality, to public service in his country.

When comparing and analyzing the two provisions, they share many similarities, but the relevant provision of the Covenant is much more precise: it directly stipulates the right to be elected.

Regarding European human rights instruments, the core text of the European Convention on Human Rights (ECHR) does not contain any provision regarding political participation as neither the right to vote nor the right to be elected are guaranteed in this legal document. The Protocol No. 1 to the Convention (1952), however, aimed to fill this gap by regulating the right to free elections in its Article 3:

> The High Contracting Parties undertake to hold free elections at reasonable intervals by secret ballot, under conditions which will ensure the free expression of the opinion of the people in the choice of the legislature.

The quoted ECHR provision ceases to directly regulate the issue in detail as it does not explicitly mention either universal and equal suffrage or the right to vote and to be elected, contrary to the relevant provisions of the UN human rights documents. Also, this provision's wording is formulated so it does not contain the guarantee of the right to free election but does include the duty of the state to hold free elections.

However, the European Court of Human Rights (ECtHR) played a significant role in developing this provision through its case law. In its first decision based on the Article 3 of Protocol No. 1 in case Mathieu-Mohin and Clerfayt v. Belgium from 1987, the Court interpreted this provision, establishing the principles of the guaranteed rights and their protection. Accordingly, the Court first held that the formulation used in this provision ("The High Contracting Parties undertake"), which differs from the formulations used elsewhere in the Convention (like "Everyone has the right"), implies that this adjustment does not establish any rights for individuals.

Later interpretation of the Preamble and the relation between the different Convention amendments and protocols confirmed that the guarantee contained in this provision includes individual rights as well. In determining those rights, the Court followed the latter opinion of the Commission that mandated the rights enshrined in Article 3 of Protocol No. 1 to include the right to vote and to stand for elections. These rights are not absolute, and states have a wide margin of appreciation.

Other regional human rights regimes' legal documents additionally contain relevant provisions. Article 23 of the American Convention on Human Rights (ACHR), which was adopted in 1978, guarantees the right to vote and to be elected and regulates on which basis these rights can be limited:

> 1. Every citizen shall enjoy the following rights and opportunities:
> a. to take part in the conduct of public affairs, directly or through freely chosen representatives;
> b. to vote and to be elected in genuine periodic elections, which shall be by universal and equal suffrage and by secret ballot that guarantees the free expression of the will of the voters; and
> c. to have access, under general conditions of equality, to the public service of his country.
> 2. The law may regulate the exercise of the rights and opportunities referred to in the preceding paragraph only on the basis of age, nationality, residence, language, education, civil and mental capacity, or sentencing by a competent court in criminal proceedings.

The African Charter on Human and Peoples' Rights (AfCHPR), adopted on June 27, 1981 and entered into force in 1986, has a provision about the right to participate in government (Article 13), like the provision of the Universal Declaration:

> 1. Every citizen shall have the right to participate freely in the government of his country, either directly or through freely chosen representatives in accordance with the provisions of the law.
> 2. Every citizen shall have the right of equal access to the public service of his country.
> 3. Every individual shall have the right of access to public property and services in strict equality of all persons before the law.

The right to be elected has been developed mainly through jurisprudence of regional and international judicial human rights institutions. Generally, the right to be elected is guaranteed to everyone with the existing eligibility requirements remaining reasonable and non-discriminative. This also includes the eligibility of candidates, which requires procedural fairness. Some of the standards adopted require the state to take measures that ensure opportunities to exercise the right to be elected, proportionate and appropriate conditions for candidates, non-arbitrary and fair mechanisms for the counting of votes, and just and impartial procedures in case of electoral misconduct. Still, these bodies acknowledge that every state's historical and political evolution must be respected while implementing conditions for exercising the right to be elected.

Johns mentions the "robust" right to be elected to describe the scope of this right. She claims that the content of this right consists of everyone's potential to be a political candidate and includes two duties of states — a positive and negative one. A negative duty on a state refrains from imposing unjustifiable eligibility requirements on candidates for elective office to protect the core right to be qualified, not the rights of those qualified. Consequently, a state can place restrictions on eligibility only if a strong justification of these restrictions is provided. Positive duty concerns the procedural dimension of the right — general equality of opportunities among potential candidates shall be secured through the establishment of a fair electoral framework within which the right may be exercised.

As expressed, the right to be elected can be directly or indirectly guaranteed in human rights documents, with the number of states accessing and ratifying these documents being quite high. The next section will explore how states integrated the guarantees from global and regional documents into their own constitutional texts.

1.5. Guarantee of the Right to be Elected in Comparative Constitutional Law

Domestic regulations evidently do not follow international standards on regulating the right to be elected. Most constitutions do not contain provisions regarding the right to be elected, and only some have provisions concerning the right to vote. The guarantee and enjoyment of this human right is often regulated by laws and other legal documents and therefore, are more prone to change and manipulation.

Modern constitutions usually contain sections with basic rights and freedoms listed, which give an idea of the fundamental rights and the different levels of importance each holds. The remainder of this section critically analyzes if, and how often, the right to be elected is found in contemporary constitutions in the world.

Using the existing database of the constitutions of the world (Constitute Project), 192 constitutions currently in force have been analyzed. Of these constitutions, only 135 contain provisions regarding universal suffrage, and only 32 countries contain provisions guaranteeing the right of citizens to be elected.

In her work, Johns analyzed 150 constitutions and found that 27% contained a provision regarding the right to be elected while provisions of other constitutions had "a more general right to hold public office or to directly participate in government, from which a right to candidacy may conceivably be derived" (Johns 2016, 32). Concordantly, Johns found that 66% of the analyzed constitutions had no provision concerning the right to be elected.

The following table contains the analyzed countries, listed alphabetically, whose constitutions contain provisions regarding the right to be elected, referring to the number of relevant provisions and their texts, as indicated below.

Table 1 Provisions concerning right to be elected in the constitutions

Country	Relevant provision	Text of provision
Albania (1998, rev. 2016)	Part II, Chapter 3, Article 45	Every citizen who has attained the age of 18, even on the date of the elections, has the right to elect and be elected.
Andorra (1993)	Title IV, Chapter 1, Article 51	All Andorran nationals fully enjoying their political rights are entitled to vote and to be eligible for election.
Angola (2010)	Title II, Chapter 2, Section 1, Article 54	Every citizen who has attained the age of eighteen years shall have the right to vote and stand for election for any state or local authority body and to serve their terms of office or mandates, under the terms of the Constitution and the law.
Bahrain 2002 (rev. 2017)	Chapter I, Article	e. Citizens, both men and women, are entitled to participate in public affairs and may enjoy political rights, including the right to vote and to stand for elections, in accordance with this Constitution and the conditions and principles laid down by law. No citizen can be deprived of the right to vote or to nominate oneself for elections except by law.
Cambodia (1993, rev. 2008)	Chapter III, Article 34	Khmer citizens of either sex shall enjoy the rights to vote and to stand as candidates for an election.
Canada (1867, rev. 2011)	Part I, C, 3 (Democratic rights of citizens)	Every citizen of Canada has the right to vote in an election of members of the House of Commons or of

		a legislative assembly and to be qualified for membership therein.
Congo (2005, rev. 2011)	Title I, Chapter I, Section 2, Article 5	Without prejudice to the provisions of Articles 72, 102 and 106 of this Constitution, all Congolese of both sexes, of eighteen years of age [at least], and enjoying their civil and political rights are electors and eligible, under the conditions determined by the law.
Egypt (2014)	Chapter III, Article 87	The participation of citizens in public life is a national duty. Every citizen has the right to vote, run in elections, and express their opinion in referendums. The law shall regulate the exercise of these rights. Performance of these duties may be exempted in cases specified by the law.
Ethiopia (1994)	Chapter III, Part II, Article 38, line 1c	Every Ethiopian national, without any discrimination based on colour, race, nation, nationality, sex, language, religion, political or other opinion or other status, has the following rights: […] c. To vote and to be elected at periodic elections to any office at any level of government; elections shall be by universal and equal suffrage and shall be held by secret ballot, guaranteeing the free expression of the will of the electors.
Fiji (2013)	Chapter 2 (Bill of Rights), Article 23	3. Every citizen who has reached the age of 18 years has the right a. to be registered as a voter; b. to vote by secret ballot in any election or referendum under this Constitution;

		c. to be a candidate for public office, or office within a political party of which the citizen is a member, subject to satisfying any qualifications for such an office; and d. if elected, to hold office.
Gambia (1996, rev. 2004)	Chapter IV, Article 26	Every citizen of The Gambia of full age and capacity shall have the right, without unreasonable restrictions- […] b.to vote and stand for elections at genuine periodic elections for public office, which election shall be by universal and equal suffrage and be held by secret ballot;
Germany (1949, rev. 2014)	Chapter II, Article 28, line 1 and Chapter III, Article 38, line 2	The constitutional order in the Länder must conform to the principles of a republican, democratic and social state governed by the rule of law, within the meaning of this Basic Law. In each Land, county, and municipality the people shall be represented by a body chosen in general, direct, free, equal, and secret elections. In county and municipal elections, persons who possess citizenship in any member state of the European Community are also eligible to vote and to be elected in accord with European Community law. In municipalities a local assembly may take the place of an elected body. (38)2. Any person who has attained the age of eighteen shall be entitled to vote; any person who has attained the age of majority may be elected.

Honduras (1982, rev. 2013)	Title II, Chapter III, Article 37, line 1	The following are rights of citizens: 1. To vote and be elected;
Hungary (2011, rev. 2016)	Article XXIII, line 1	Every adult Hungarian citizen shall have the right to vote and to be voted for in elections of Members of the National Assembly, local government representatives and mayors, and of Members of the European Parliament.
Iraq (2005)	Section II, Chapter I, Article 20	Iraqi citizens, men and women, shall have the right to participate in public affairs and to enjoy political rights including the right to vote, elect, and run for office.
Kenya (2010)	Article 38.3 (Political Rights)	Every adult citizen has the right, without unreasonable restrictions a. to be registered as a voter; b. to vote by secret ballot in any election or referendum; and c. to be a candidate for public office, or office within a political party of which the citizen is a member and, if elected, to hold office.
Kosovo (2008, rev. 2016)	Chapter II, Article 45, line 1	Every citizen of the Republic of Kosovo who has reached the age of eighteen, even if on the day of elections, has the right to elect and be elected, unless this right is limited by a court decision.
Lesotho (1993, rev. 2011)	Chapter II, Article 20, line 1	Every citizen of Lesotho shall enjoy the right: [...] b. to vote or to stand for election at periodic elections under this Constitution under a system of universal and equal suffrage and secret ballot;
Malawi (1994, rev. 1999)	Chapter IV, Article 40, line 3	Save as otherwise provided in this Constitution, every person shall have the right to vote, to do so in

		secret and to stand for election for public office.
Marshall Islands (1979, rev. 1995)	Article II, Section 14	Every person has the right to participate in the electoral process, whether as a voter or as a candidate for office, subject only to the qualifications prescribed in this Constitution and to election regulations which make it possible for all eligible persons to take part.
Mongolia (1992, rev. 2001)	Chapter II, Article 16, line 9	The citizens of Mongolia shall be guaranteed to exercise the following rights and freedoms: […] 9. The right to participate in State management [public administration] affairs directly or through the organs of representation. Have the right to elect and to be elected to the State organs. The right to elect shall be exercised from the age of eighteen years, and the age qualification for being elected shall be determined by law, taking into consideration the requirements for the relevant State organs and official positions concerned.
Netherlands (1815, rev. 2008)	Chapter 1, Article 4	Every Dutch national shall have an equal right to elect the members of the general representative bodies and to stand for election as a member of those bodies, subject to the limitations and exceptions prescribed by Act of Parliament.
New Zealand (1852, rev. 2014)	Part 2, Subpart 2, Article 12	Every New Zealand citizen who is of or over the age of 18 years a. has the right to vote in genuine periodic elections of members of the House of Representatives, which

		elections shall be by equal suffrage and by secret ballot; and b. is qualified for membership of the House of Representatives.
Palestine	Title Two, Article 26	Palestinians shall have the right to participate in political life, both individually and in groups. They shall have the following rights in particular: [...] 3. To vote, to nominate candidates and to run as candidates for election, in order to have representatives elected through universal suffrage in accordance with the law.
Rwanda (2003, rev. 2015)	Chapter 1, Article 2	Suffrage is universal and equal for all Rwandans. All Rwandans, both men and women, fulfilling the requirements provided for by law, have the right to vote and to be elected.
Serbia (2006)	Part 2, 2, Article 52	Every citizen of age and working ability of the Republic of Serbia shall have the right to vote and be elected.
Somalia (2012)	Chapter 2, Title 2, Article 22	2. Every citizen who fulfils the criteria stated in the law has the right to elect and to be elected.
South Africa (1996, rev. 2012)	Chapter II, Article 19, line 3b	3. Every adult citizen has the right a. to vote in elections for any legislative body established in terms of the Constitution, and to do so in secret; and b. to stand for public office and, if elected, to hold office.
South Sudan (2011, rev. 2013)	Part 2, Article 26, line 2	Every citizen shall have the right to vote or be elected in accordance with this Constitution and the law.
Sudan (2005)	Part 2, Article 41, line 2	Every citizen shall have the right to stand for elections in periodic

		elections, which shall be by universal adult suffrage and shall be held by secret ballot, guaranteeing the free expression of the will of the electorate.
Turkey (1982, rev. 2017)	Chapter IV, Part II, Article 67	In conformity with the conditions set forth in the law, citizens have the right to vote, to be elected, to engage in political activities independently or in a political party, and to take part in a referendum.
Zimbabwe (2013, rev. 2017)	Chapter 4, Article 67, line 3	Subject to this Constitution, every Zimbabwean citizen who is of or over eighteen years of age has the right a. to vote in all elections and referendums to which this Constitution or any other law applies, and to do so in secret; and b. to stand for election for public office and, if elected, to hold such office.

While analyzing relevant provisions of the constitutions, my aim was to identify those which guarantee the right to be elected. Additionally, I searched for provisions that ensure this right to all citizens of the country, without any limits or reservations as unreasonable restrictions on this right is unacceptable in democracy. These limits will be discussed in greater detail in the next section.

Johns argues that the constitutional provisions regarding the composition of government, or more generally, the eligibility criteria for candidates of major elective offices, are representative of Dworkin's "enabling" constitutional rules, which serve to construct a majority government by stipulating the terms and conditions of elections. These rules, though not explicitly found in the texts, allow eligible citizens to claim their right to be elected. Johns argues that these provisions should be made explicit rather than left vague, found in all constitutions, and guaranteed to all adult citizens without any state-justified limitation of the right (Johns 2016, 32). The state, therefore, has a duty not only to guarantee the right to be elected to everyone, but also to guarantee equal access to the right to all its citizens. Johns calls this a "robust" conception of the right to be elected (Ibid, 33).

Another reason for the need of an explicit provision concerning the right to be elected is its tight connection to the democratic political system of a state. Only states whose constitutions contain provisions regarding elementary democratic structures can be considered democratic because these structural provisions that determine the set-up of a democratic system must be constitutional, constant and "immune to change" (Schneider 2000, 104-105). Otherwise, the political system of a country, whose constitution does not contain such provisions, risks no longer being considered a democracy (Ibid).

1.6. Limitations of the Right to be Elected

Electoral rights are usually the line of differentiation between the citizens and non-citizens. Although electoral rights can be granted to resident aliens or non-citizen residents, generally, this is not the case. Traditionally, electoral rights are the exclusive privilege of citizens of one country, and some countries even make a difference between citizen residents and non-resident citizens.

The analysis of the constitutional guarantees of electoral rights showed that while the constitutions of many countries in the world guarantee universal suffrage or the right to vote, they also do not contain a guarantee of the right to be elected. This is problematic as it devalues this right's importance, categorizing it as a less valuable right, even with regulation, and thereby making it easier to change the requirements for this right's enjoyment at any moment.

Historically, race and gender were common restriction criteria in the enjoyment of electoral rights. This helps explain why some countries emphasize gender equality in electoral rights' regulations. Constitutional provisions of five states exemplify this gender equality significance in the enjoyment of the right to be elected: Cambodia, the Congo, Ethiopia, Iraq, and Rwanda. Ethiopia's constitution, for example, emphasizes the enjoyment of the right without discrimination based on sex in addition to color, race, nation, nationality, language, religion, political or other opinion or other status.

While limiting both the right to vote and the right to be elected to adult citizens capable of basic reasoning and rationality skills is widely accepted as reasonable, there is a difference in age regulation as a condition for the enjoyment of the electoral rights. The provisions of eight states' constitutions—Albania, Angola, Congo, Fiji, Kosovo, Mongolia, New Zealand, Zimbabwe—prescribe the age of eighteen years as a condition for every citizen to vote and be elected. This age limitation is regarded reasonable and acceptable as only persons at the age of eighteen are considered to have the capacity to respect these rights and obligations. It is especially important to emphasize here that the age limitation is determined for both active and passive suffrage, which indicates that both rights are accepted as co-equal rights.

In many other countries, the age limitation for the enjoyment of the right to vote and right to be elected differs. While the right to vote at the national presidential and legislative elections is limited to citizens of the age of sixteen or eighteen (except for Italy, where the age for voting for the Chamber of Deputies and Senate is twenty-five), the right to be elected differs, ranging from eighteen to forty years of age. Meanwhile, lower-level elections—regional and municipal elections—stipulate, as expected, a younger age limit, varying between sixteen and thirty years of age.

Provisions in other states' constitutions refer to age in different ways. While Gambia refers to legal age as "full age" and Germany as "age of majority", Hungary and South Africa label it "adult". There are also cases in which determining the age for enjoyment of the right to be elected are decided by laws and/or other legal acts. These are potentially dangerous situations because the age condition is not precise, risking easier and less formal legislation amendments and thereby restricting or completely forbidding the enjoyment of the right to be elected. Such a limitation on the guarantee of the right to be elected renders said guarantee false. An example of this provision appears in Article 27 of the Constitution of Tajikistan:

> "After having attained the age of 18 years, a citizen has the right to participate in a referendum, to vote, and also to become elected after having attained the age established by the Constitution, constitutional laws, and laws."

The provisions of some of the analyzed constitutions refer to legislative documents that decide the conditions for the enjoyment of the right to be elected. Namely, the limitations and exceptions to the right to be elected should be:

- determined by the law (Title I, Chapter I, Section 2, Article 5 of the Constitution of Congo, Chapter IV, Part II, Article 67 of the Constitution of Turkey),

- regulated by the law (Chapter III, Article 87 of the Constitution of Egypt),
- limited by the court decision (Chapter II, Article 45, line 1 of the Constitution of Kosovo),
- election regulations (Article II, Section 14 of the Constitution of Marshall Islands), or
- be decided by acts of parliament (Chapter 1, Article 4 of the Constitution of the Netherlands).

These limitations make the guarantee of the right to be elected to all citizens potentially "empty" and "superficial". However, even this restricted type of guarantee can still be accepted as these provisions, at least principally and declaratively, guarantee the right to be elected to all citizens.

Beside these, common restrictions in the enjoyment of the right to vote and to be elected include mental disability, criminal offence, restrictions, and limitations for members of army, police, judges, clergy, and dual and naturalized citizens. The norms concerning mandatory voting and remote voting can also be considered a type of limitation in the enjoyment of the electoral rights.

2. Protection of the Right to be Elected in the European Convention on Human Rights — Case Study of Bosnia and Herzegovina

2.1. The Protection of the Right to be Elected in Bosnia and Herzegovina

States with a homogenous population are rare, and the most important challenges today are guarantees of equal citizens' rights in addition to the protection of minorities and their rights. Power-sharing arrangements are a common solution for these issues in divided societies, and consociationalism, along with federalism and centripetalism, are prominent types of power-sharing arrangements that address the management of places divided by nationality, ethnicity, language, religion, and other powerful non-class cleavages (Lijphart 1977).

Bosnia and Herzegovina, after the 1992-1995 war and signing of the Dayton Peace Agreement, became a typical (corporate) consociation (McCrudden and O'Leary 2013). This peace agreement represented a huge milestone not only for the peace building process in Bosnia and Herzegovina and its overall history, but also for the UN's peace building efforts, which included rebuilding of civil society, strengthening the rule of law, police restructuring, judicial and penal reform, monitoring human rights, elections, media regulation, and tackling corruption (Chandler 2017, 68). While the Annex IV to the Dayton Peace Agreement serves as the country's constitution in force, Annex VI, the Agreement on

Human Rights, and a few other annexes like those concerning elections, the restoration of the infrastructure and the settlement of the disputes between the entities, also have a "constitutional dimension" (Morrison 1996, 145) and an importance comparable to the Dayton Constitution (Steiner and Ademović 2010, 19), effectively characterizing the whole peace agreement as "a constitution in the broadest sense" (Bell 2006, 392).

With its ambitious human rights protection, the Dayton Peace Agreement had potential to provide a basis for the country's development but turned out to be the biggest obstacle to the country's progress as it failed to "provide a blueprint for a functional state" (Keil and Kudlenko 2015, 482). The outlined general framework for some institutions and its core elements were contradictory and paradoxical, resulting in a lack of progress in state-reconstruction. The country's only progression occurred between 1997 and 2006, a period marked by intensive international intervention and imposition. The country's stagnation began in 2006 and continues today.

The Dayton Constitution provides that Bosnia and Herzegovina is a "democratic state, which shall operate under the rule of law and with free and democratic elections" (Dayton Constitution, Article II). This provision establishes Bosnia and Herzegovina as a democratic state, committed to the principles of rule of law and free and democratic elections, but it does not specify the type of democracy founded. The emphasis on the rights of the three constituent peoples and "a vast amount of autonomy over the territory in which they were the majority" (Keil and Kudlenko 2015, 483) implies that this is the type of democracy which only serves the interests of the constituent peoples, who elect their own elites for the purpose of cooperating and working together in postwar Bosnia. At the same time, the Dayton Constitution foresaw a liberal democracy which protects the rights of the constituent peoples, while also guaranteeing human rights to all citizens, no matter their ethnic origins or place of residence. These contradictory aims have proven unachievable in practice, at least in the current setting in Bosnia and Herzegovina.

The relationship between the state and its entities and the relationship between the entities themselves is "deliberately left ambiguous" (McCrudden and O'Leary 2013, 21). The high level of decentralization makes Bosnia and Herzegovina "a very loose union" (Bieber 2006, 40). It represents a triple power-sharing system, with power-sharing mechanisms in the entities and cantons as well as at the state level (Ibid, 44), thereby adhering to condition for a classic corporate consociation (McCrudden and O'Leary 2013, 21) and a "controlled democracy" (Bojkov 2003, 42). It is a hybrid regime with both democratic institutions and mechanisms and non-democratic ones. However, it is not clear whether Bosnia and Herzegovina is a (asymmetric) federation, confederation or federalizing state. It is "at least a federation" (Bieber 2006, 60), imposed federation (Keil 2013, 102), or imposed consociation (Merdzanovic 2015).

Initially, when the DPA was signed, power-sharing mechanisms, which included all three constituent peoples and Others as a separate category, existed only at the state level, as prescribed by the Dayton Constitution, while entities represented two exclusive territories of some constituent peoples—the Republika Srpska, the exclusive territory of Serbs, and the Federation of Bosnia and Herzegovina, the exclusive territory of Bosniacs and Croats. The Dayton Constitution required compliance with the constitution and gave entities the responsibility to amend their constitutions within three months, but this provision of the constitution was neglected and not implemented by the entity authorities. This discord was removed by the Constitutional Court of Bosnia and Herzegovina's decision in four parts, in which many provisions of entities' constitutions were declared unconstitutional (Constitutional Court of BiH, Decision No. U-5/98).

The European Commission for Democracy through Law, better known as the Venice Commission, confirmed this decision, emphasizing that Bosnia and Herzegovina, as a multinational state, could not justify assimilation or segregation of any ethnic group. The fact that one of the constituent peoples might be in a majority or minority position in the entities was put aside by the constitutional recognition of all three people as equal, meaning that none of them are constitutionally recognized as a majority, or in other words, that they enjoy equality as groups. This principle, consequently, can also be interpreted as a prohibition of "any special privilege for one or two of these peoples, any domination in governmental structures or any ethnic homogenization through segregation based on territorial separation" (Venice Commission 2001, 4).

Upon the local politicians' reluctance to implement this "landmark decision" (Morawiec-Mansfield 2003, 2066), the High Representative appointed constitutional commissions in both entities. Based on the commissions' proposals and negotiations between the local politicians, the Mrakovica Agreement was reached on March 27, 2002. The agreement contained principles that stipulated constitutional changes in both entities to provide legitimacy of all three constituent peoples in both entities and their proportional representation in government and public administration at all levels, based on the 1991 census that determined the representation quota. The National Assembly of Republika Srpska adopted a different version of the amendments, which were in accordance with the Constituent Peoples decision but not with the Mrakovica Agreement. This reflected the situation in the Federation, where certain resistance to amendments also emerged. As a result, the High Representative Wolfgang Petritsch imposed the constitutional amendments in both the Federation of Bosnia and Herzegovina and Republika Srpska. In this way, "ethnic power-sharing mechanisms" (Keil 2013, 95) were introduced to the whole territory of Bosnia and Herzegovina, but this also made the mono-national/bi-national political systems of the entities much more complex and lacking a reduced predominance of nationalist interests. These constitutional changes secured formal ethno-national balance at the entity level, but not at the municipality level or in public companies. Only after these amendments did Bosnia and Herzegovina "[become] a consociation (in an empirical sense) on all of its levels" (Merdzanovic 2015, 289).

The implementation of this important decision was possible only when the OHR intervened and established the needed institutions. The country's bogus post-war progress also was the result of the High Representative's decisions. The system established by the Dayton Constitution was pushed aside every time the High Representative had to intervene, and power-sharing arrangements and their fundamental principles like reciprocity and consensual decision-making were ignored and undermined (Keil 2013, 107). A political culture of consensus and reciprocity was consequently not developed; ethno-nationalist parties not only continued with their nationalistic rhetoric and firm attitudes, but they also did not have to justify complicated decisions to their electorate, instead blaming the High Representative for imposed decisions. At the same time, this fostered a climate where the respect for human rights and minorities was pushed away by the interests of the ethnic elites. Obviously, the system established in Dayton was not functional from the very beginning, making its reform was inevitable.

The serious international discussions for the constitutional reform in BiH started in 2004, with the Council of Europe Parliamentary Assembly's Resolution 1384 ("Strengthening of democratic institutions in Bosnia and Herzegovina") and continued first with the Venice Commission's Opinion and followed by the European Court of Human Rights decision in the case Sejdić and Finci v. Bosnia and Herzegovina.

Upon Bosnia and Herzegovina's acceptance in the Council of Europe in 2002, the Parliamentary Assembly of the Council of Europe on June 23, 2004, authorized the Venice Commission to create a comprehensive assessment of the conformity of the Constitution of Bosnia and Herzegovina with the Convention for the Protection of Human Rights and Fundamental Freedoms and the European Charter of Local Self-Government (ETS No. 122). This assessment examined the efficiency and rationality of the present constitutional arrangements in Bosnia and Herzegovina and the compliance of the High Representative's authorities with the Council of Europe's basic principles and ECHR. The Commission noted the complexity and oddities of the Dayton Constitution, correctly identified the state's most pressing issue with the implementation of the power dispersal at many levels in a small territory, and the emerging issues. It found the competencies given to the central state extremely narrow and insufficient for a country's progress towards European integration. The constitutional reform was found inevitable for many reasons in addition to the comprehensive and sudden transfer of responsibilities, including executive agencies and a decrease of bureaucracy. Consequently, a decrease of the High Representative's intervention and a formal change visible in constitutional text were recommended. Few provisions of the Dayton Constitution and subsequent institutions were declared clear obstacles for BiH both becoming a functional state and respecting the Council of Europe's standards and ratified human rights documents, which required the vital national interest veto, the House of Peoples, and the Presidency. In conclusion, the Commission proposed concrete steps to be implemented as the part of the constitutional changes in Bosnia and Herzegovina. As a medium and long-term goal of the country's constitutional reform, this process included: a transfer of responsibilities from the Entities to central state by means of amendments to the Dayton Constitution; a streamlining of decision-making procedures within Bosnia and Herzegovina, especially with respect to the vital interest veto; a reform of the provisions on the composition and election of the Presidency and the House of Peoples, the territorial re-organization of Bosnia and Herzegovina — i.e., concentration of legislative responsibilities within the Federation of Bosnia and Herzegovina at the entity level and strengthening of local government in both entities and the change of the emphasis from a state based on the equality of three constituent peoples to a state based on the equality of citizens.

This perspective has been extremely important for two primary reasons. Firstly, it finally highlighted all the shortcomings of the system established by the Dayton Constitution. Secondly, it emphasized the need for the elimination of discriminative provisions and offered the viable solutions to those changes. It became a kind of reference and starting point for all further debates on constitutional changes, as it correctly identified all the problems of the current system. It also proposed "soft", however substantial, reforms to the Dayton constitution instead of "hard" reforms that would involve a new territorial order in Bosnia and Herzegovina (Keil 2013, 142).

Soon after the opinion, an American initiative called the "Dayton Constitutional Project" emerged with the proposals concerning constitutional reform in Bosnia and Herzegovina. This was "the only serious, albeit modest, attempt to move beyond the Dayton settlement" (Bennett 2015, 172), but unfortunately it never progressed far. Through the US Embassy in Sarajevo, the nine-month long process involved discussions between heads of the country's eight most important political parties and the three-man secretariat, chaired by Don Hays, US diplomat and former principal deputy high representative. The aim was to conclude negotiations and reach an agreement about reforms to be voted on in the state parliament by March 2006, so the changes could enter into force before the general elections scheduled for October 2006. During the negotiations, representatives from the Party for Bosnia and Herzegovina (SBiH), and later the Croatian Democratic Community (HDZ), the leading Croatian party in Bosnia and Herzegovina, strongly disagreed with some of the proposed solutions concerning the issue of "entity voting" and withdrew from the negotiations. The constitutional reform proposal that was sent to parliament for voting was significantly different than the initial one but still covered main problematic issues of the current system. However, the so-called "April Package" failed on April 26, 2006, to gain the required two-third majority in the House of Representatives by only two votes.

The following two initiatives, known as Prud Process and Butmir Process, were doomed to fail as they clearly indicated inconsistency of the meaning and the content of the constitutional reform for Bosnian politicians. The first initiative represented a mere declarative commitment of leaders from the three biggest ethnic parties in Bosnia and Herzegovina regarding constitutional changes. The Butmir Process, initiated by the US and the EU, consisted of two meetings held in October 2009 among the representatives of seven of the eight parties that were part of the negotiations about the April package. The negotiation team included experienced diplomats and officials, and the constitutional amendment proposal included all necessary elements indicated in previous proposals. In the end, the Butmir talks failed due to timing, their unnecessary rush, over emphasis of EU integration versus financial incentives, and poor preparations (Bennett 2015, 207). However, the main reason for the failure was in fact that "the Bosnian leaders had mutually incompatible visions of their country and no incentive to compromise" (Ibid). Both initiatives showed once again that there was no minimum compromise on the meaning and content of constitutional changes.

The Dayton Constitution gives exceptional importance to human rights and democracy. Some of the human rights are explicitly listed in the Constitution's provisions while others are only considered guaranteed through the interpretation of preamble. To correctly interpret the meaning, it is necessary to understand the preamble's importance in relation to the DPA's legal nature. The DPA is an international treaty with the preamble accordingly viewed as part of the treaty. Consequently, the Dayton Constitution is an integral part of DPA, implying that the Preamble is also an integral part of the Constitution, albeit with normative characteristics (Steiner and Ademović 2010, 37). The first line of the Preamble mentions the respect for human dignity as the basis of the Constitution, followed by the values of liberty and equality also positioned as the "fundamental and central constitutional values" (Steiner and Ademović 2010, 37). The state's main task is to protect and guarantee these values as is reflected in other provisions of the Dayton Constitution concerning human rights, such as Article II and X.2 and Annex 1. The concept of human dignity is not defined, so it is left open to interpretation.

The eighth line of the Preamble lists the Universal Declaration of Human Rights, the International Covenants on Civil and Political Rights and on Economic, Social and Cultural Rights, the Declaration on the Rights of Persons Belonging to National or Ethnic, Religious and Linguistic Minorities, and other important human rights documents as the Dayton Constitution's inspiration. The texts detailed in the DPA, Annex 1 (not containing the Universal Declaration of Human Rights) and the wording in the Preamble affirms the respect for human rights, in particular the rights of minorities, emphasizing the importance of the regional and global human rights documents.

In Article II, the Dayton Constitution regulates human rights and freedoms. Exceptional importance is given to human rights in the Dayton Constitution, Article II.1 stating that "the highest level of internationally recognized human rights and fundamental freedoms" is guaranteed. This eliminates any kind of discrimination, especially in the context of the European Human Rights Convention and its protocols.

The provision in Article II.2 of the Dayton Constitution might be considered one of the most important constitutional provisions regarding human rights because it assigns direct application of the European Convention in Bosnia and Herzegovina and its priority over all other law. This provision's importance was especially high before Bosnia and Herzegovina ratified the European Convention and became a member of the Council of Europe. Its interpretation created a dilemma: was this provision applicable only to law and other regulations, or to the Dayton Constitution itself as well? The Constitutional Court declared that it is not in its competence "to decide in the present case on the conformity of certain provisions of the Constitution of BiH with the European Convention and its Protocols" (Constitutional Court of BiH, 2006), and that the European Convention entered into force through the Constitution of Bosnia and Herzegovina, thereby deriving its constitutional authority from the Constitution of Bosnia and Herzegovina and not from the European Convention itself (Ibid).

Begić explains that the European Convention was intended to be applied in Bosnia and Herzegovina "only partially by virtue of its Constitution" (Begić 2016, 13) while the direct application and priority over all other law in application of the European Convention and its Protocols meant that all legal acts had to be in accordance with the Convention, excluding the Constitution. The real intention of the constitution makers behind the discussed provision may have needed to establish certain human rights protection standards, combined with the country's uncertain progress towards achieving membership status at the Council of Europe and ratification of the European Convention, which helps explain why it was left ambiguous. In this way, the European human rights standards would be applicable even without formally signing the Convention. Steiner and Ademović share a similar opinion, stating that the constitution makers aimed "to automatically, in an 'ultra-monistic' manner, introduce into the national legal system the necessary international law related to fundamental human rights and freedoms, to avoid, amid divergent national interests, the complicated procedure of enacting laws" (Steiner and Ademović 2010, 177).

The provision of the Article II.3 enumerates some of the human rights protected. The expression used in this provision, and in the proceeding provisions, indicates that it was intended as an exemplary, not exclusive, list of human rights. All other human rights and fundamental freedoms guaranteed and protected in the human rights documents listed, either in the Dayton Constitution or in Annex I, should be equally protected.

Although the right to vote and the right to be elected are not listed in this provision, the Dayton Constitution indirectly protects them. Consequently, the provision of Article 3 of Protocol No. 1 to the European Convention of Human Rights shall be directly applied and have priority over the discriminative provisions of Articles IV(1), IV(1)(a), IV(3)(b) and V(1) of the Dayton Constitution. However, provisions of the Dayton Constitution and other legal acts in the country explicitly show that the right to be elected is limited to certain categories of people. This is especially the case with the provisions of the Dayton Constitutions concerning the election of the members of Presidency and the House of the Peoples. The restrictions existed in the entities until the implementation of the Constitutional People decision, when all constituent people formally became represented in both entities.

The Election Law of Bosnia and Herzegovina is one of the most important legal documents concerning the right to be elected, which contains provisions for organizing and implementing elections as well as the election results. With its numerous amendments, this controversial law's provisions, especially those concerning the distribution of positions in legislative and executive powers, are highly important. The Election Law in Article 1.4. prescribes:

> Each citizen of Bosnia and Herzegovina who attained eighteen years of age shall have the right to vote and right to be elected (further: electoral rights), in accordance with the provisions of this law. To exercise this right, a citizen must be registered as a voter, in accordance with this law.

Furthermore, the Election Law stipulates certain restrictions on the right to vote, to be elected and to participate in a political party in elections (Article 1.6 to 1.8 of the Election Law). For example, a person serving a prison sentence ascertained by the International Criminal Tribunal for the former Yugoslavia for war crimes or failure to comply with the order and appear before the Court cannot register to vote, be a candidate of the elections, or hold any appointive, elective, or other public position in the territory of Bosnia and Herzegovina. In the event such a person holds a position or function in a political party or coalition, that party or coalition is deemed ineligible to participate in the elections (Article 1.6). The restrictions not only apply to the International Tribunal, but also to decisions from the Court of Bosnia and Herzegovina, the Court of the Federation of Bosnia and Herzegovina, the Court of Republika Srpska and the Court of Brčko District of Bosnia and Herzegovina. It also applies to proceedings in other countries, where the International Tribunal for the former Yugoslavia has reviewed the file prior to arrest and found that it meets international legal standards, and in the cases of serious breach of the international humanitarian law (Article 1.7 and 1.7.a).

Furthermore, a person can only become a candidate if they previously resigned from their position as a judge of regular and Constitutional courts, prosecutor, deputy, attorney, Ombudsmen, Member of the Human Rights Courts/Chambers/Councils, notary, member of police forces, civil servant, member of the Armed Forces of BiH, member of the Intelligence and Security Agency, or diplomatic and consular representative of Bosnia and Herzegovina abroad (Article 1.8).

From the analysis of these provisions, it is apparent that universal suffrage is guaranteed in Bosnia and Herzegovina, with an age restriction of 18 years, which is accepted as a reasonable limitation. There are certain restrictions placed on exercising the right to be elected in some categories, and they are accepted as reasonable given the short amount of time that passed after the war, the unsuccessful reconciliation process in the country, and the extensive crimes that were committed in Bosnia and Herzegovina.

Article 8.1, in accordance with Article V of the Dayton Constitution, determines the election of members of the Presidency of Bosnia and Herzegovina. Following the territorial principle of the constitutional norm, Bosniac and Croat members to the Presidency are elected from the Federation of Bosnia and Herzegovina and Serb members to the Presidency from the Republika Srpska. Members of the Presidency can only come from the different constitutive peoples elected territorially but cannot be exclusively elected by the voters of their own ethnic group. However, Article 8.1 states that voters in the Federation of Bosnia and Herzegovina can vote either for a Bosniac or Croat candidate, independent of whether they are Serb or a member of some minority group (Others), whereas voters in Republika Srpska can only vote for one of the Serb candidates, even if they are Bosniac, Croats or Others.

This provision has been especially problematic for Croats as Croats are allegedly being outvoted by Bosniacs in elections for the Croat member of Presidency. For them, or rather for the Croatian Democratic Union (HDZ), the Croat member of Presidency, Željko Komšić, elected for a mandate 2006-2014 and again 2018-2022, was purportedly elected by Bosniac votes and is therefore not the legitimate representative of the Croats. There have been reactions from Croatia concerning this issue, with excessive attempts to impact the election processes in Bosnia and Herzegovina by emphasizing the need for change of the electoral law and lobbying at the EU Parliament. However, Komšić's election is both legal and legitimate under the current Constitution and laws of the country. This "Croat Question" (Merdzanovic 2015, 215) is often reflected in the claims that Croats in the Federation are being discriminated against, deprived of their rights, outvoted, etc. This issue, together with the provisions about the elections of the members of the House of Peoples in the Parliament of Federation of Bosnia and Herzegovina, are the Election Law provisions Croats insist on amending. Allegedly, the disputed provisions enable cantons with a Bosniac majority to dominate in terms of representation, and the number of elected delegates does not reflect the number of Croat people living in those cantons, thus inaccurately representing Croat interests.

Following these claims and upon filing the application, the Constitutional Court of Bosnia and Herzegovina asked the opinion on this issue from the Venice Commission. The Commission (Venice Commission 2016) emphasized that election legislation shall be accepted as the state's competence, and that the second legislative chamber in Bosnia and Herzegovina has an important role, therefore proposing amendment of the Election Law norm regarding the seat allocation of the House of Peoples, as stated in the Constitution of the Federation.

The Court brought the decision on December 1, 2016 and decided that the provision of Article 10.12 (2) — according to which each of the constituent peoples shall be allocated one seat in every canton — the provisions of Chapter 20 — Transitional and Final Provisions of Article 20.16A (2) — and items a-j of the Election Law of Bosnia and Herzegovina were not in conformity with Article I (2) of the Constitution of Bosnia and Herzegovina. The Constitutional Court of Bosnia and Herzegovina ordered the Parliamentary Assembly to implement the decision in six months. When it failed to do so, the disputed provisions of the Election Law were repealed, creating a legal loophole. The amendment procedure was supposed to end six months prior to the general elections in 2018 so that the new provisions of the law would be applicable. When the necessary amendments were not adopted and the earlier Constitutional Court's decision in the case U-23/14 was not implemented, the Constitutional Court on July 6, 2017, decided to end the disputed provisions of the Election Law.

The general elections were held on October 7, 2018. The election's results, however, were not implemented, and the government, at both the central and federal levels, did not form for more than three months after the elections. It was suggested that the 2018 election and its results could be implemented without any problem even without amending the Election Law (ESI 2018), and the Central Election Commission on December 18, 2018, issued a Direction on Change and Amendments of the Direction on Implementation of Indirect Election for the Government Institutions under the Election Law of Bosnia and Herzegovina. This way, the 2018 elections were implemented but the issue remained problematic for Croats in Bosnia and Herzegovina and their representatives kept insisting on amending election legislature.

The country's complicated constitutional settings are best reflected in the electoral system chosen and applied in Bosnia and Herzegovina. It is a proportional representation system with open party lists. The country's division into electoral units, the complicated distribution of mandates and the existence of the compensation mandates, together with indirect election of members of the House of People at both state and entity levels, make voters' roles in choosing their representatives illusionary. Additionally, there are serious suspicions about electoral manipulations, even for the candidates on the same party list. And although the electoral legislative in Bosnia and Herzegovina *de lege lata* is far from ideal, it is important to bear in mind the many significant amendments that have already been made to the Election Law, some imposed by the High Representative and others by the Constitutional Court's decisions. Hence, additional constitutional amendments are inevitable in making this post-war country truly democratic, especially considering that one of the most important aspects of these amendments concerns the regulation reform of the right to be elected within the European standards.

The right to be elected, otherwise referred to by the ECtHR as the right to stand for elections, was introduced in the

European Human Rights system with Protocol No. 1, or more precisely, through case law and interpretation of the right to free elections from Article 3 of Protocol No. 1. A case law concerning this right only started to develop towards the end of the 1970s and beginning of the 1980s, with many decisions brought in the 1990s concerning the post-Soviet states. A modest number of cases might have been the result of the interpretation of the right and widely accepted principle of the states' margin of appreciation.

The ECHR's preamble states that fundamental freedoms, which represent the foundation of justice and peace in the world, can best be obtained by an effective political democracy. Although the interpretation of Article 3 of the Protocol No. 1 restricts the right to be elected only to the legislature, it is of great significance and accepted as one of the fundamental rights protected by the ECHR.

The interpretation of Article 3 has shaped the right to free elections, including the right to stand for elections, as maintained in this provision. In that sense, the Court's rulings in cases Mathieu-Mohin and Clerfayt v. Belgium (§§ 48-51), Ždanoka v. Latvia (§ 102), Podkolzina v. Latvia (§ 35), Melnitchenko v. Ukraine (§ 57), Riza and Others v. Bulgaria (§ 142), and Davydov and Others v. Russia (§§ 284-285) were especially notable. As time has gone on, the European democracy standards have been established.

Although legislative power is not restricted to parliament, the power given to local authorities in many countries to make regulations and by-laws is distinguished from the legislative power of the parliament. Subsequently, the provision of Article 3 does not cover local, municipal, or regional elections. However, the application of this provision to the presidential elections is not totally excluded, at least theoretically (ECtHR, Boškoski v. the Former Yugoslav Republic of Macedonia, 2004). In every single case, the ECtHR examines the constitutional structure of the state, its functions, and its role as an institution to determine how the legislative power of the concerned state is exercised. Regarding the organizations of elections, it is important to point out that states have a wide margin of appreciation in deciding a reasonable number of intervals for holding elections, in addition to having power to address other issues.

Although the wording of Article 3 seems restrictive, there has been a significant number of cases concerning this provision (total of 119 cases). This provision deals with various aspects of the right to free elections including: the right to vote (restrictions on the right to vote because of national origin, citizens living abroad, persons placed under protection, or prison), the eligibility (formal conditions of eligibility, disqualification due to prior conduct or affiliations, disqualification based on ethnical origin), voting irregularities, electoral systems, and media coverage of elections. All these decisions have been further shaped by the election systems and electoral rights in Europe.

The provision's literal interpretation indicates that a certain right for individuals is not established, but rather an obligation for states is created. In regard to the preparatory work in respect of Article 3 of Protocol No. 1 and the interpretation of the provision in the context of the Convention as a whole, the Court has established that this provision also implies individual rights, comprising the right to vote (the "active" aspect) and to stand for election (the "passive" aspect) (Council of Europe, 2020, 6-7).

Hence, the margin of appreciation is left to states, enabling them to prescribe certain restrictions to these rights.

These "implied limitations" are not precise in the provision, as seen in Articles 8 to 11 of the ECHR which dictates that every state is "free to rely on an aim not contained in that list to justify a restriction, provided that the compatibility of that aim with the principle of the rule of law and the general objective of the Convention is proved in the particular circumstances of a given case" (Ibid). Based on this, the ECtHR had been deliberating over "whether there has been arbitrariness or a lack of proportionality, and whether the restriction has interfered with the free expression of the opinion of the people" (Ibid).

The electoral legislation of every country has been analyzed considering its own historical context and political evolution, and as a result, one system's unacceptable characteristics risk misled acceptance and justification in the electoral system of another country.

The right to free elections additionally concerns the post-election period, namely, the counting of votes and the recording and transmission of the results. A state is obliged to ensure that the processes logging and translating the votes are implemented carefully.

Regarding the right to complain about or report alleged violations, the Court accepted that in addition to individuals, political parties whose candidates' rights had been violated can also independently claim to be victims. In one of the more prominent cases, Podkolzina v. Latvia, the Court interpreted the right to stand for elections as "inherent in the concept of a truly democratic regime" (§35). In this decision the Court established standards for the enjoyment of this right, stipulating that one cannot be arbitrarily deprived of the right to be elected at any moment and that this right can be limited only after finding a candidate has failed to comply with several criteria in place to prevent unreasonable decisions. Furthermore, the judgment in question must be reached by a body which can provide a minimum guarantee of impartiality as well as "discretion...[that] must not be exorbitantly wide", but "circumscribed, with sufficient precision, by the provisions of domestic law". At the same time, "the procedure for ruling a candidate ineligible must be guaranteed a fair and objective decision and prevent any abuse of power on the part of the relevant authority" (Ibid). The standards from this Court's decision, if applied properly, would indeed serve in securing a transparent and fair procedure, and consequently, ensure the right to stand for elections.

Additionally, the Court found violations of the right to stand for elections in several other cases, including:

- the termination of the mandate of Members of Parliament because of the dissolution of their party by the Constitutional Court (Sadak and Others v. Turkey),
- the refusal to register a candidate in parliamentary election (Melnychenko v. Ukraine),
- the immediate application during the current parliamentary term of provision disqualifying those engaging in professional activities from sitting as MPs (Lykourezos v. Greece),
- the illegitimate and unjustified exclusion of two electoral districts from the country-wide vote tally (Georgian Labour Party v. Georgia),
- the inability of persons with multiple nationalities to stand as a candidate in parliamentary elections (Tănase v. Moldova),
- the permanent ineligibility of an impeached President to stand for election to parliamentary office (Paksas v. Lithuania),

- a member of parliament prevented from discharging his duties because of his prolonged pre-trial detention, without a proper examination of the possibility of alternative measures (Selahattin Demirtaş v. Turkey).

Quantitatively, most of the applicants in ECtHR cases concerning the right to be elected are from Azerbaijan (19), Turkey (9), Bosnia and Herzegovina (6), Italy (4), and Latvia (4). In four of the cases, a violation of Article 3 of Protocol No. 1 was found in connection with Article 14 of the ECHR (Prohibition of the discrimination) — Sejdić and Finci v. Bosnia and Herzegovina, Zornić v. Bosnia and Herzegovina, Danis and Association of Ethnic Turks v. Romania, and Šlaku v. Bosnia and Herzegovina. Additionally, the Court also found the discrimination in the enjoyment of the electoral rights in Bosnia and Herzegovina in three more cases: Pilav v. Bosnia and Herzegovina, Baralija v. Bosna and Herzegovina, and Pudarić v. Bosnia and Herzegovina. The discrimination in these cases was based on the provision of Article 1 of Protocol No. 12.

The ECtHR's rulings concerning the discrimination in the enjoyment of the right to be elected in BiH emphasize the most crucial shortcoming of the system established by the Dayton Constitution: while declaratively having developed human rights protection, it systematically continues to discriminate many of its citizens, specifically in enjoyment of their electoral rights. The ECtHR finding regarding the protection of the right to be elected in BiH further stressed the non-logic of the declarative commitment of the Dayton Constitution with respect for human rights and racial discrimination embedded within it. They confirm that the current system in Bosnia and Herzegovina is prejudiced against minorities and citizens who do not want to be affiliated with any of the three ethnic groups or the constituent peoples. Decisions in the cases Sejdić and Finci v. Bosnia and Herzegovina, Zornić v. Bosnia and Herzegovina, Šlaku v. Bosnia and Herzegovina, Pilav v. Bosnia and Herzegovina, Baralija v. Bosnia and Herzegovina, and Pudarić v. Bosnia and Herzegovina are some of the most significant milestones in postwar Bosnia and Herzegovina and for the general prohibition of discrimination in Europe.

The first case in which the Court ruled originated from the two separate applications filed in July and August 2006 that later merged and were judged together as one case in front of the Court. Both applicants, Dervo Sejdić and Jakob Finci, are members of national minorities (Roma and Jewish communities), and consequently did not declare affiliation with any of the constituent peoples. Both applicants have held important public positions and actively participated in the public life of the state. However, because of not declaring themselves as members of one of the three constituent people, they were not able to stand for elections as a member of the House of Peoples of the Parliamentary Assembly or the Presidency of Bosnia and Herzegovina. For this reason, both filed complaints of being discriminated against in the election process.

The applicants' claims in the first case alleged violations of Article 3 of Protocol No. 1 to ECHR, Article 14 ECHR in conjunction with Article 3 of Protocol No. 1 to ECHR, and Article 1 of Protocol No. 12 to ECHR in relation to their inability to be elected to the House of Peoples and Article 1 of Protocol No. 12 to ECHR in relation to their inability to be elected to the BiH Presidency. The violation of Article 14

ECHR in conjunction with Article 3 of Protocol No. 1 to ECHR regarding the applicants' inability to be elected to the House of Peoples and Article 1 of Protocol No. 12 to ECHR in relation to their inability to be elected to the BiH Presidency were declared.

The applicant in the second case, Ms. Azra Zornić, is a citizen of Bosnia and Herzegovina who refused to declare her affiliation with any of the three constituent peoples or national minorities, simply declaring herself a citizen of Bosnia and Herzegovina and actively participating in the country's political life. She was therefore deprived of her candidacy rights and not able to stand for elections as a member of the House of Peoples of the Parliamentary Assembly or the Presidency of Bosnia and Herzegovina. Ms. Zornić complained of her ineligibility to stand for election to the House of Peoples and Presidency. She also relied on the same provisions as the applicants in the first case.

The applicant's complaints in the second case are identical to those of the applicants in the Sejdić and Finci v. Bosnia and Herzegovina case. In both cases the applicants' alleged violation was founded on the same legal basis and provisions of the ECHR. However, the cases differed in respect to the applicants' non-affiliation with the constituent peoples. While Sejdić and Finci were affiliated with the Roma and Jewish national minorities, Zornić refused to affiliate with any constituent peoples, identifying herself as a BiH citizen only. The Dayton Constitution neither recognizes citizens as a separate category nor ascribes them any specific rights under the current constitutional settings, so the individual in question is classified as Others, meaning anyone who is not affiliated with the constituent peoples and thereby directly considered as a minority.

In Zornić's case the violation of Article 14 ECHR in conjunction with Article 3 of Protocol No. 1 to ECHR and Article 1 of Protocol No. 12 to ECHR regarding the applicants' inability to be elected to the House of Peoples and Article 1 of Protocol No. 12 to ECHR in relation to her inability to be elected to the BiH Presidency were declared.

The third case's applicant Amir Šlaku is a member of the Albanian minority in Bosnia and Herzegovina, who has worked in the Ministry for Human Rights and refugees and actively in the NGO sector (his father was one of the founders of the Association of Albanians in Bosnia and Herzegovina – Klub Albanaca). Except for this applicant's identification as another minority ethnic group in BiH, the Court found this case "identical to Sejdić and Finci" (§29). Both the violation of Article 14 ECHR in conjunction with Article 3 of Protocol No. 1 to ECHR and Article 1 of Protocol No. 12 to ECHR regarding the applicants' inability to be elected to the House of Peoples and Article 1 of Protocol No. 12 to ECHR in relation to his inability to be elected to the BiH Presidency were declared.

The applicant in the fourth case, Ilijas Pilav, is a Bosniac medical doctor who was born and lived in Srebrenica, Republika Srpska his whole life and who was socially and politically active in the local community at the entity level for years. Nevertheless, because of the territorial and ethnic restrictions concerning the elections to the Presidency, he could not become a member of the Presidency of Bosnia and Herzegovina. In other words, just because he was a Bosniac living in Republika Srpska, he could not be elected to BiH Presidency. Pilav repeatedly claimed discrimination based on ethnic origin and emphasized the combination of both the ethnical and territorial principles, which made it impossible for him to exercise his rights.

Pilav claimed, and the Court declared, violation of Article 1 of Protocol No. 12 to ECHR regarding his inability to be elected to the BiH Presidency.

The case of Baralija vs. Bosnia and Herzegovina differs from previous cases in its focus on local elections but is similar in that the alleged violation relates to the discrimination of enjoyment of both the right to vote and right to be elected. Ms. Irma Baralija, president of the local branch of Naša Stranka, was born in 1984 and lives in Mostar, the biggest city in the Herzegovina region and the region's cultural and economic capital. During the war, the city was divided, and although the Croatian and Bosniac division is in the past, the city's integration in practice is disputable. According to the City of Mostar Statute adopted in 2004 upon the imposition by the High Representative, the city consists of six areas which correspond to abolished municipalities and are also electoral units (city area electoral constituencies), together with the sixth city electoral unit (a city-wide electoral constituency). The Statute further determined that three city councilors be elected from five electoral units and 17 councilors from the sixth area. The Election Act 2001 identically regulated this issue, however, problems emerged when Croats claimed that these provisions enabled the electoral areas with lower populations to be represented by the same number of councilors, an action that is not in accordance with the international electoral standards. The Constitutional Court confirmed this in its decision, ordering it to be changed in six months.

Due to the non-implementation of the Constitutional Court of Bosnia and Herzegovina's decision No. U-9/09, the provisions of the Election Act as well as the Statute of the City of Mostar were put out of force by the consecutive decision of this judicial body. Consequently, and because of the impossibility of reaching a compromise on the necessary legal reforms concerning the election of the members of Mostar City Council, the local elections were not held for almost ten years. The city, therefore, was governed by the last elected mayor, who had a "technical mandate" since 2012.

Ms. Irma Baralija claimed that because of this she was deprived of her right to vote and to be elected and thus unable to take a part in local self-government. The applicant further complained that her inability to vote or stand in local elections in the city of Mostar amounted to discrimination on the grounds of her place of residence and relied on Article 1 of Protocol No. 12 to ECHR (ECtHR 2019, §30). The Court found the violation of this ECHR provision in this case as well.

In the last case, applicant Svetozar Pudarić, a Bosnian Serb politician born in Sarajevo in 1959, where he lived until his death in 2020, was a member of the Socialist-democratic party (SDP BiH) and elected to various political positions, including vice-president of the Federation of BiH. In May 2018 he submitted his independent candidacy for the election to the Presidency of BiH at the general elections to be held that year. The candidacy was rejected because he was not residing in Republika Srpska, and therefore, could not be a candidate for this position, despite his being an ethnic Serb and his affiliation with this constituent people in BiH. The Court of Bosnia and Herzegovina rejected his appeal dismissing it as inadmissible. Finally, Pudarić lodged his application to the ECtHR on October 25, 2018, claiming discrimination in the enjoyment of his electoral rights, which amounted to a violation of Article 1 of Protocol No. 12. After Pudarić died, his wife decided to continue with the procedure with the Court ruling on December 8, 2020, that Article 1 of Protocol No. 12 to ECHR was violated.

Table 2 Prohibition of discrimination in conjunction with the right to be elected in Bosnia and Herzegovina – cases analysis

	Alleged violation	Admissibility	Merits	Court's decision
Sejdić and Finci v. Bosnia and Herzegovina (2009) - Racial discrimination (ethnical discrimination – members of minorities) - Ineligibility to stand for election to the House of Peoples and the Presidency of Bosnia and Herzegovina				
	House of Peoples			
	Article 14 of the ECHR in conjunction with Article 3 of Protocol No. 1	-Because of the applicants' active participation in public life they can claim to be victims of alleged discrimination; -State can be held responsible for maintaining the contested constitutional provision; -Admissible.	-Elections to the House of Peoples falls within the scope Article 3 of Protocol No. 1; -Ethnical/racial discrimination cannot be objectively justified in a contemporary democratic society.	Violation
	Article 3 of Protocol No. 1			No need to examine
	Article 1 of Protocol No. 12			No need to examine
	Presidency			
	Article 1 of Protocol No. 12	Admissible	-Provision applicable; -There is no pertinent distinction between	Violation

			the notion and amount of discrimination concerning the House of Peoples and Presidency.	
Zornić v. Bosnia and Herzegovina (2014) - Racial discrimination (ethnical discrimination – refusal to declare affiliation with any of the "constituent people"/declares as a citizen) - Ineligibility to stand for election to the House of Peoples and the Presidency of Bosnia and Herzegovina	**<u>House of Peoples</u>**			
	Article 14 of the ECHR in conjunction with Article 3 of Protocol No. 1	-Because of the applicant's active participation in public life they can claim to be victims of alleged discrimination; -State can be held responsible for maintaining the contested constitutional provision; **-Admissible.**	-The present case is identical to Sejdić and Finci; -The applicant should not be prevented from standing for elections for the House of Peoples on account of her personal self-classification.	Violation
	Article 3 of Protocol No. 1			No need to examine
	Article 1 of Protocol No. 12			Violation
	<u>Presidency</u>			
	Article 1 of Protocol No. 12		Same as in Sejdić and Finci.	Violation

	Presidency		
Pilav v. Bosnia and Herzegovina (2016) - Discrimination of the member of the „constituent peoples" (Bosniacs in RS) in some parts of the country (combination of ethnic origin and place of residence) - Ineligibility to stand for election to the Presidency of Bosnia and Herzegovina	Article 1 of Protocol No. 12	-State can be held responsible for maintaining the contested constitutional provision; -Admissible.	-Exclusion is based on a combination of ethnic origin and place of residence and as such discriminatory.	Violation
	House of Peoples			
Šlaku v. Bosnia and Herzegovina (2016) ***the case identical as the Sejdić and Finci v. Bosnia and Herzegovina***	Article 14 of the ECHR in conjunction with Article 3 of Protocol No. 1	-Because of the applicants' active participation in public life they can claim to be victims of alleged discrimination;	-The meaning of the discrimination in Article 1 of Protocol No. 12 is being identical to that in Article 14, therefore the test for its existence being the same as well; -case identical to Sejdić and Finci.	Violation
	Article 3 of Protocol No. 1			No need to examine
	Article 1 of Protocol No. 12	-State can be held responsible for maintaining the contested constitutional provision; -Admissible.		Violation

	Presidency		
	Article 1 of Protocol No. 12		Same as in Sejdić and Finci.	Violation
	City Mayor/Council (Mostar)		
Baralija v. Bosnia and Herzegovina (2019) - Territorial discrimination - Ineligibility to vote and stand for the local elections in City of Mostar	Article 1 of Protocol No. 12	- Because of her active political life, the applicant is a member of a class of people directly affected by the situation complained of, and may therefore claim to be a victim of the alleged discrimination.	- There is a legal void which has made it impossible for the applicant to exercise her voting rights and her right to stand in local elections for a long time; - territorial discrimination.	Violation
	Presidency		
Pudarić v. Bosnia and Herzegovina (2020) - Discrimination of the member of the „constituent	Article 1 of Protocol No. 12	Admissible	-Exclusion is based on a combination of ethnic origin and place of residence and as such discriminatory.	Violation

peoples" (Serbs in FBiH) in some parts of the country (combination of ethnic origin and place of residence) - Ineligibility to stand for election to the Presidency of Bosnia and Herzegovina			

2.2. The European Court of Human Rights' Evaluation of the Cases concerning the Discrimination in Enjoyment of the Right to be Elected in Bosnia and Herzegovina

Upon analysis of ECtHR cases concerning electoral rights in BiH, it is evident that all found violations are based on discrimination in the enjoyment of these rights. Therefore, it is necessary to make a few remarks about the prohibition of discrimination in the European human rights regime. Primarily, both the principles of equality and non-discrimination seek to tackle a similar issue—treating persons in similar situations in the same way. The principle of non-discrimination is accepted as "the most frequently protected principle of international human rights law" (Besson 2012, 154), but has only recently gained importance, which is also reflected in the ECtHR's case law. However, the Court's case law in this area is criticized as lacking a theoretical and doctrinal consistency (Gerards 2013, 102).

The provision of Article 14 of ECHR contains the prohibition of the discrimination clause, which provides only limited protection when compared to other international human rights protection instruments. This "odd provision" (Gerards 2013, 100) is viewed "as a minimal clause, subsidiary to national constitutional equal protection clauses" (Besson 2012, 154) and "a second-class guarantee under ECHR law" (Ibid, 159). Together with the modest caselaw (only seventy-four cases since ECHR entered into force), this provision has proven to be insufficient "to constitute a complete regime of ECHR discrimination law" (Ibid, 160) and has also resulted with "a regrettable lack of overall coherence" (Ibid) in this area. This is in part because of the prohibition's accessory character regarding other Convention provisions, as well as the fact that the Court has often chosen to decide on the violation of the right itself, not under Article 14 (Gerards 2013, 100).

The provision of Article 14 prohibited only the discrimination of the rights and freedoms guaranteed in the Convention:

> The enjoyment of the rights and freedoms set forth in this Convention shall be secured without discrimination on any ground such as sex, race, color, language, religion, political or other opinion, national or social origin, association with a national minority, property, birth or other status.

This provision outlines a wide list of prohibited discrimination acts, which are exemplary, so it is applicable if the discrimination is founded on some other grounds. At the same time, its scope is limited to the rights listed in the ECHR. The provision of Article 14 did not create an additional right, but an applicable principle if the case in question falls within the ambit of some of the rights in ECHR (Besson, 156). These rights include mostly civil and political individual rights, as well as some economic and social rights.

The case-law concerning the provision of Article 14, taken in conjunction with a substantive right can be examined even if there has been no violation of the substantive right itself. Furthermore, a complaint of discrimination can fall within the scope of some specific right, even if the specific entitlement in the ECHR does not relate to a specific issue. Still, it will be considered to fall within the scope of the ECHR indirectly through an interpretation.

While the material scope of the non-discrimination principle under Article 14 was limited and encompassed all national law concerning the rights guaranteed in ECHR, Protocol No. 12 broadened the prohibition of discrimination to all areas of national law. In its Preamble, the principle of equality before the law and equal protection by the law is emphasized as a fundamental principle, with its main objective being promoting this principle through the collective enforcement of prohibiting discrimination. The wording of the Preamble indicates the relation between the principles of equality and prohibition of discrimination. These intertwined principles ensure "equal situations are treated equally and unequal situations differently. Failure to do so will amount to discrimination unless an objective and reasonable justification exists" (Council of Europe 2000, 11). The Preamble's third line refers to measures taken to promote full and effective equality, which obliges states to adopt and implement anti-discriminatory laws and then ensure they are respected in practice.

Prescribed general prohibition of discrimination in Article 1 stipulates the following:

> The enjoyment of any right set forth by law shall be secured without discrimination on any ground such as sex, race, color, language, religion, political or other opinion, national or social origin, association with a national minority, property, birth, or other status.
>
> No one shall be discriminated against by any public authority on any ground such as those mentioned in paragraph 1.

The first paragraph of Article 1 is almost identical to Article 14 of the ECHR with the only difference occurring in the words "by law" in the provision of Article 1. The rights and freedoms set forth in the Convention are to be protected from discrimination, while in the provision of Article 1, enjoyment of the rights set forth by the law and by any public authority are those for which the discrimination is prohibited. This nuanced difference between the two almost identical provisions changed the whole system of prohibition of discrimination in the European human rights regime.

This way, a general non-discrimination clause was introduced, and the scope of the protection from discrimination was extended beyond the rights and freedoms guaranteed in the ECHR to all rights guaranteed in the national legislations of the countries which sign and ratify the Protocol No. 12. For these countries, a principle of equality before and in the law was introduced (Besson 2012, 155). With Article 1 of Protocol No. 12, the prohibition of discrimination became a free-standing right under the ECHR and a self-standing non-discrimination principle (Ibid, 152). With this, now a general and independent non-discrimination principle is guaranteed. The scope of the protection covers persons facing discrimination in the following instances:

- in the enjoyment of any right specifically granted to an individual under national law.
- in the enjoyment of a right which may be inferred from a clear obligation of a public authority under national law, that is, where a public authority is under an obligation under national law to behave in a particular manner.
- by a public authority in the exercise of discretionary power (for example, granting certain subsidies).
- by any other act or omission by a public authority (for example, the behavior of law enforcement officers when controlling a riot).

To conclude, the prime objective of this provision is to embody a negative obligation—to not discriminate against individuals. In the second paragraph, the prohibition of discrimination by public authorities is also emphasized. The term has been used before by the ECHR, referring to "not only administrative authorities but also the courts and legislative bodies" (Council of Europe 2000, 6). However, the protection of individuals from discrimination is also applicable in the relationships between private persons, which should normally be regulated by the state but are delegated to private persons in some cases. In Article 2 of the Protocol, it prescribes the territorial application of the general prohibition of discrimination.

Due to the similarities and at times overlapping between Article 14 of the ECHR and Article 1 of the Protocol No. 12, questions of applicability may arise. However, Article 1 of Protocol No. 12 is the provision of an additional Protocol. Therefore, it does not amend or abrogate Article 14 of the ECHR, but rather it is considered an additional Article to the Convention (Article 3 of Protocol No. 12) for the States which signed and ratified the Protocol No. 12. For these states, there is a possibility of an eventual overlap between the two provisions. Article 32 of the ECHR prescribes that if any matter or question of interpretation and application arises, or the precise relationship between the provisions of the Convention and the protocols is uncertain, the final decision falls within the jurisdiction of the Court. In the event there is a need for protection from discrimination of the right that is guaranteed by the Convention, it is expected that the provision of Article 14 of the ECHR will be applied. If the relevant right is not guaranteed by the ECHR, then Article 1 of Protocol No. 12

shall be applied. Of course, this also depends on how the applications are formed and the applicants' claims in each case.

Usually, applicants allege the violation of Article 14 in conjunction with some substantive right guaranteed in the ECHR. If the Court finds a violation of Article 14, it will not examine the complaint of violation of substantive right, as it would basically involve the review of the same complaint. This is how the Court proceeded in deciding in the Sejdić and Finci case and the other analyzed cases concerning the violation of the right to be elected to the House of Peoples in Bosnia and Herzegovina.

Ruling in the Sejdić and Finci case indicated that the Court does not assess whether Protocol No. 12 has been violated if Article 14 is applicable. Yet, it is worth mentioning as it has not been commented on in other literature that the Court ruled opposite in the Zornić and Šlaku cases. Namely, applicants in all three cases complained about the violation of Article 14 in conjunction with Article 3 of Protocol No. 1 and violation of Article 1 of Protocol No. 12 regarding the ineligibility to be elected to the House of Peoples of the Parliamentary Assembly of Bosnia and Herzegovina. In the first case, the Court found the violation of Article 14 of the ECHR in conjunction with Article 3 of Protocol No. 1 regarding the election to the House of Peoples, concluding that there was no need to examine the alleged violation of the Article 1 of Protocol No. 12 regarding the same issue. In two following cases, which differed from the first one in the reasons for applicants' non-affiliation with the constituent peoples but were identical in the applicants' complaints of the alleged violations, the Court found a violation of the Article 14 of the ECHR in conjunction with Article 3 of Protocol No. 1 and a violation of the Article 1 of Protocol No. 12 regarding the election to the House of Peoples. This change in the Court's decision was poorly explained and left room for different interpretations of the relation between the two ECHR provisions concerning the protection from discrimination.

The Protocol No. 12 to ECHR was adopted on November 4, 2000 and entered into force in the ten member-states on April 1, 2005. Bosnia and Herzegovina was among the first countries to sign and ratify the Protocol. When it entered into force, it also became applicable in the country. Approximately a year later, the first case was registered, which claimed an alleged violation of Article 1 of the Protocol No. 12 against Bosnia and Herzegovina. The case attracted a lot of attention, primarily because it was the first case where the new standard of the prohibition of discrimination was applied. Second, it represented a case which had the potential of shattering the whole system established by the Dayton Peace Agreement.

The restrictive constitutional provisions regarding the election of members of the House of Peoples and Presidency impose twofold restrictions to candidates—they must be members of a certain constituent people and come from a certain part of the country. In the first three cases, the ethnic aspect of the restriction was emphasized because the applicants were not affiliated with any of the constituent people, while in the fourth and sixth case, another territorial dimension of discrimination in the constitutional provisions was emphasized.

The important issue common for all the analyzed decisions is the issue of affiliation with one of the constituent peoples. In its Preamble, the Dayton Constitution makes the distinction between the constituent peoples (Bosniacs, Croats and Serbs, along with Others) and citizens (DPA 1995). In theory, all these groups are equally positioned in relation to the constitution, but in practice, members of other ethnic groups, national minorities and the citizens in general are not equally situated with the members of the constituent peoples in Bosnia and Herzegovina. The Constitutional Court of Bosnia and Herzegovina confirmed this decision as legal and constitutional (Constitutional Court 2000), thereby confirming the attitude that "the Constitution of Bosnia and Herzegovina determines that Bosniacs, Croats and Serbs are the architects-framers of the Constitution" (Steiner and Ademović 2010, 61) while the Others and citizens are systematically deprived of their rights.

A significant dimension of this issue is the declarative nature of an individual's ethnic affiliation. Because the Dayton Constitution has no provision to determine one's ethnicity, this issue is not legally regulated and thus, self-classification is widely accepted as a proper mode of determination. This mode, however, is prone to abuse and changes. For example, the Election Law of Bosnia and Herzegovina prescribes that the candidate lists shall contain, among others, a "declared affiliation with a particular constituent people or the group of Others" (Election Law of BiH 2000, Article 4.19.(4)).

The same provision explains that the declaration of one's affiliation is the basis for determining whether a person has the right to stand as a candidate for certain positions, and without it, shall be eliminated in the election process. The determination of a person's ethnic affiliation was similar in the former Yugoslavia—declarative self-classification with no objective conditions to be fulfilled such as knowing the language, or belonging to a certain religion, etc.

The provisions concerning the election of members of the House of the Peoples and the Presidency of Bosnia and Herzegovina contain obvious restrictions for members of national minorities and the citizens who do not declare their affiliation with one of the three constituent peoples, particularly regarding certain parts of the country's territory. The relevant provisions of the Dayton Constitution are Article IV and Article V. Article IV.1 of the Dayton Constitution prescribes the composition of the House of Peoples:

> The House of Peoples shall comprise 15 Delegates, two-thirds from the Federation (including five Croats and five Bosniacs) and one-third from the Republika Srpska (five Serbs).

To be eligible for a member of the House of Peoples, one must declare himself either as a Croat or Bosniac and must be living in the Federation of Bosnia and Herzegovina, or he must declare himself as a Serb and living in Republika Srpska. A Serb from the Federation of Bosnia and Herzegovina cannot be a member of the House of Peoples just as a Croat or Bosniac living in Republika Srpska cannot be a member of this legislative body. The situation is identical to the election to the Presidency of Bosnia and Herzegovina. The relevant provision combines both the ethnic and territorial principle in the process of the election for this executive state organ. Article V of the Dayton Constitution regulates the election of the members of Presidency of Bosnia and Herzegovina:

> The Presidency of Bosnia and Herzegovina shall consist of three Members: one Bosniac and one Croat, each directly elected from the territory of the Federation, and one Serb directly elected from the territory of the Republika Srpska.

The cited provisions contain ethnic and territorial restrictions and are consequently discriminating against those who do not affiliate with one of the constituent peoples.

In the case evaluation process, the ECtHR considered the case in the light of international law and referred to different legal documents of the United Nations, Council of Europe, EU and OSCE. Namely, the Court invoked provisions of Article 5 of the International Convention on the Elimination of All Forms of Racial Discrimination, Articles 2(§1), 25 and 26 of the International Covenant on Civil and Political Rights, and opinions and reports of the Committee on the Elimination of Racial Discrimination, Venice Commission, European Commission against Racism and Intolerance (ECRI), the OSCE Office for Democratic Institutions and Human Rights and European Commission. The referred provisions prohibit racial discrimination in an election process. All the mentioned opinions and reports warn of the existence of discriminative constitutional provisions, emphasizing the applied discriminatory practices and condemning them.

Discussing the admissibility issues required the Court to decide whether the applicants are indeed victims of discrimination, and whether the respondent state should be held responsible for the alleged violation. The applicants "must be directly affected by the impugned measure" (ECtHR 2009, §29), not simply contest the provisions of the national law in relation to the ECHR. In deciding these issues, the ECtHR in Sejdić and Finci v. Bosnia and Herzegovina case took a stand that the applicants may claim to be victims of alleged discrimination. Because of their active participation in public life, "it would be entirely coherent that they would in fact consider running for the House of Peoples or Presidency" (Ibid). The Government did not object to this.

Bardutzky argues that in the situation where the issue concerns an impugned prohibitive legislative provision "there is no need to individualize the affected person in order to establish his status as a victim: all persons that belong to the Others can be considered victims of these provisions" (Bardutzky 2010, 325). He finds the Court's argument on the applicants' active engagement in public life and their likelihood to consider running for elections dubious (Ibid).

To determine the state's responsibility for alleged violations, the Court highlighted specific issues in the Bosnia and Herzegovina constitution. These circumstances include, namely, the mere existence of the constitution as the annex to an international treaty and the peace agreement itself. Furthermore, the Court, without discussing whether the state is responsible for implementing contested constitutional provisions, ruled that "it could nevertheless be held responsible for maintaining them" (ECtHR 2009, § 30), as only the Parliamentary Assembly of Bosnia and Herzegovina has the power to amend the Constitution.

In discussing the cases, the applicants claimed that the factual situation represented ethnic discrimination, a form of racial discrimination. This type of discrimination is "not capable of justification and amount[s] to direct discrimination" (Ibid, §32). Its difficulty in justification arises because of the area in which it is applied: political participation and representation at the highest level of state.

The government argued that it "enjoyed considerable latitude in establishing rules within their constitutional order to govern parliamentary elections and the composition of the parliament" (Ibid, §34). It further asserted that "the time was still not ripe for a political system which would be a simple reflection of majority rule" (Ibid).

The Court first examined the applicability of the relevant ECHR provisions in cases of the alleged violations concerning the House of Peoples of the Parliamentary Assembly of Bosnia and Herzegovina. The applicants relied on Article 14 of the Convention in conjunction with Article 3 of Protocol No. 1, Article 3 of Protocol No. 1 taken alone, and Article 1 of Protocol No. 12 in the allegation of the violation concerning the House of Peoples, as well as violation of Article 1 of Protocol No. 12 to ECHR concerning the Presidency of Bosnia and Herzegovina.

Assessing the case, the Court restated that the provision of Article 14 ECHR "has no independent existence since it has the effect solely in relation to 'the enjoyment of the rights and freedoms' safeguarded by those provisions" (ECtHR 2009, § 39). Nevertheless, this provision extends to the rights which are not explicitly listed in the ECHR, namely "those additional rights falling within the general scope of any Convention article, for which the State has voluntarily decided to provide" (Ibid). It was found that the provision of Article 3 of Protocol No. 1 is applicable only to elections of a legislature, whereas the legislature must be interpreted in every single case concerning the state's "constitutional traditions and the scope of the legislative powers of the chamber in question" (Ibid, §40). In that sense, and with the respect to the bicameral design of most states' parliaments and general rule of the ineffectiveness of the second chamber, the Court took a stand that the provision of Article 3 of Protocol No. 1 is "carefully drafted so as to avoid terms which could be interpreted as an absolute obligation to hold elections for both chambers in each and every bicameral system" (Ibid). However, it still considered this provision applicable "to any of a parliament's chambers to be filled through direct elections"

(Ibid). In relation to this, the Court concluded that the House of Peoples of Bosnia and Herzegovina, although being composed through indirect elections, enjoys extensive legislative powers concerning the passage of legislation. Without the approval of this chamber state's budget, international obligations and the treaty ratification cannot be completed. Because of all these powers, the Court decided that the elections for the House of Peoples of Bosnia and Herzegovina fell within the scope of the Article 3 of Protocol No. 1 (Ibid, § 41).

Another issue is whether there was discrimination in the election process for the House of Peoples. In assessing this issue, the Court referred to its previous stance on the meaning of discrimination—"treating differently, without an objective and reasonable justification, persons in similar situations" (Ibid, § 42). The eventual different treatment would be justified if the distinction pursued a legitimate aim or there was a reasonable relationship of proportionality between the means employed and the aim to be achieved. The ECtHR corroborated that discrimination on the account of a person's ethnic origin is a form of racial discrimination, in which case "the notion of objective and reasonable justification must be interpreted as strictly as possible" (Ibid, § 44), but also that "no difference in treatment which is based exclusively or to a decisive extent on a person's ethnic origin is capable of being objectively justified in a contemporary democratic society built on the principles of pluralism and respect for different cultures" (Ibid). In other words, the Court considered ethnic discrimination unacceptable in democratic countries, especially in Europe.

Although the country's progress has not always been consistent, it has been significant and there have been important steps indicating the country's commitment to achieve the relevant international standards in different areas. The power-sharing mechanisms peculiar to Bosnia and Herzegovina do not necessarily have to be abolished, but rather evolve to end the exclusion of ethnic groups other than the constituent peoples. The Court emphasized the country's progress concerning membership in the Council of Europe and in signing the Stabilization and Association Agreement with the EU, its voluntary acceptance of certain standards, and the implementation and integration of them into the country's system. Because of all these facts, the existing distinction cannot have an objective and reasonable justification and therefore represents a breach of Article 14, taken in conjunction with Article 3 of Protocol No. 1. The Court did not find it necessary to examine violations under Article 3 of Protocol No. 1 alone and Article 1 of Protocol No. 12.

The Presidency of Bosnia and Herzegovina cannot be considered a legislative body of the state (ECtHR 2016b, § 43), so the applicants could not claim the same violation of the ECHR provisions, as seen in the case of the ineligibility to stand for the election for the House of Peoples. That is why the applicants, in all three cases analyzed, opted for the same claim of a violation regarding their ineligibility for the election to Presidency of Bosnia and Herzegovina — Article 1 of Protocol No. 12. The Court accepted this provision applicable in the first case and followed that stand in two others as well.

The Court emphasized the character of the provision, the general prohibition of discrimination, and the meaning of the term discrimination being the same in both provisions, no matter the difference of the scope in Article 14 of the ECHR and Article 1 of Protocol No. 12. The Court found the provisions concerning the election to the Presidency both discriminatory and a breach of Article 1 of Protocol No. 12.

Described as "remarkably brief for such an important case" (McCrudden and O'Leary 2013, 93), the decision in the Sejdić and Finci case was the first case in which the decision was based on Article 1 of Protocol No. 12. The Court was criticized for failing to make clear what the provision's phrase "set forth by the law" means; confusion arose as to whether the phrase refers only to the rights established in the domestic law of the state or also to the rights guaranteed by the international law (Bardutzky 2010, 329).

In her concurring and partly dissenting opinion, judge Mijović reasons that ethnic affiliation in Bosnia and Herzegovina is not an objective and legal category but a subjective and political one, which gains importance only if an individual desires to get involved in politics. Further, she emphasized her disappointment with the Court's rather poor interpretation of Article 1 of Protocol No. 12, giving the impression that this provision is applicable only because Article 14 is not. The Court's more detailed discussion on the necessity of a tripartite structure, present in many other institutions in the country, would be much more useful in the current case, but also in relation to the future case law related to this provision.

Judge Mijović challenged the Court's stance concerning the characterization of the House of Peoples, highlighting the way members of this body are appointed/designated/selected (but not elected) and the nature of this chamber as an important element to be considered when distinguishing this political body from other similar bodies. She asserts that the list of candidates is not announced during an electoral campaign or at any other moment before the appointment and that there are no criteria that candidates for membership in this chamber of the Parliamentary Assembly of Bosnia and

Herzegovina have to fulfill to be appointed. Because of this, there is no general right for anyone to stand for election to the House of Peoples. She claims that the House of Peoples cannot even be considered a second chamber but only part of the Parliamentary Assembly of Bosnia and Herzegovina, with an exclusive task of defending the interests of constituent peoples. Judge Mijović defines the House of Peoples as a *sui generis* mechanism and arguing that "the right of any individual to stand for election to the House of Peoples per se simply does not exist in domestic law; the House of Peoples is a non-elective organ, having neither the typical characteristics nor the powers of a second chamber, and its structure places it outside the ambit of Article 3 of Protocol No. 1" (ECtHR 2009). She also questioned the state's progress, stressing the reality of the country's current social and inter-ethnical relations.

Judge Bonello criticized the way in which the Court assumed the role of deciding on the issues concerning an international peace treaty. He argued that the Court had deliberately neglected the country's and region's past. Furthermore, he contests the Court's findings the country's progress and current political situation is correct, claiming that "it is not for the Court to establish, by a process of divination, when the transitional period is over, or when a state of national emergency is past, and everything is now business as usual" (Ibid). This implies the Court's jurisdiction in the specific case of Bosnia and Herzegovina is limited.

The Court's second decision reaffirmed its stance regarding the applicants' admissibility in the Sejdić and Finci case. Meanwhile, in the Zornić case, the Government objected the victim status of the applicant, claiming that the applicant could not be considered actively involved in political life, as she only once was a candidate in the elections for Parliament of the Federation of Bosnia and Herzegovina and did not win a seat. Moreover, she was entitled to declare herself one of the constituent peoples, and while she could change her mind at any time, she still chose, by her very own will, to refrain from that proclamation. In defense, the Government representative claimed that the applicant could change her self-classification, declare the affiliation with one of the other constituent peoples, and consequently, enjoy her right.

The applicant's claims were the same as in the first case: violation of Article 14 of the Convention in conjunction with Article 3 of Protocol No. 1, Article 3 of Protocol No. 1 taken alone, and Article 1 of Protocol No. 12 in the alleged violation concerning the House of Peoples, as well as violation of Article 1 of Protocol No. 12 to ECHR concerning the Presidency of Bosnia and Herzegovina.

Although the applicant's claims in this case were the same as in case Sejdić and Finci v. Bosnia and Herzegovina, the verdict was changed. In the case of Zornić v. Bosnia and Herzegovina, the Court found both violation of Article 14 in conjunction with Article 3 of Protocol No. 1 and a violation of the Article 1 of Protocol No. 12 regarding the elections for the House of Peoples. While the Court did not state why it found it necessary to declare the applicability and violation of both Article 14 of the Convention and the Article 1 of Protocol No. 12, the Court's decision could be understood as an attempt to interpret the latter provision as a qualified type of discrimination in cases of especially unacceptable exclusionary practices.

Regarding the ineligibility to stand for the election to the Presidency, the Court relied on the previous decision, validating the found violations in this case as well (ECtHR 2014, §§ 36-37).

Furthermore, in the Zornić v. Bosnia and Herzegovina case, the Court decided to examine the application of Article 46 of the Convention as well. This implies that the Court was indeed aware of this case's complexity and considered the claimed violation more severe and a direct result of failing to implement the Sejdić and Finci case decision (§ 40). The Court additionally asserted that "more than eighteen years after the end of the tragic conflict, there could no longer be any reason for the maintenance of the contested constitutional provisions" (§ 43), and that "the time has come for a political system which will provide every citizen of Bosnia and Herzegovina with the right to stand for elections to the Presidency and the House of Peoples of Bosnia and Herzegovina without discrimination based on ethnic affiliation and without granting special rights for constituent people to the exclusion of minorities or citizens of Bosnia and Herzegovina" (Ibid).

There was one partly dissenting opinion to this ruling from Judge Wojtyczek, who criticized the applicability of the provision of Article 3 of Protocol No. 1 to the House of Peoples. He argued that the specific wording of this provision, although inclusive of both the right to vote and to be elected, could be understood in a more restrictive way in the case of second chambers elections and therefore, could claim the existence of "neither a subjective right to vote nor a subjective right to stand in elections to this chamber".

In the third case, which is identical to the first one in facts and applicants' claims, the Court did not decide the same way as in the case of Sejdić and Finci v. Bosnia and Herzegovina. Namely, concerning the violation of the applicant's right to be elected to the House of Peoples and the discrimination in the enjoyment of this right, the Court found the violation of both Article 14 ECHR in conjunction with Article 3 of Protocol No. 1 to ECHR and the violation of Article 1 of Protocol No. 12 to ECHR. As in the case of Zornić v. Bosnia and Herzegovina, the Court did not explain this reasoning in detail, only stating that "the Court concludes that there has been a violation of Article 14 taken in conjunction with Article 3 of Protocol No. 1 and a violation of Article 1 of Protocol No. 12 resulting from the applicant's continued ineligibility to stand for election to the House of Peoples of Bosnia and Herzegovina" (ECtHR 2016, § 29). The Court previously concluded that although the scope of the provisions of Article 14 and Article 1 of Protocol No. 12 were different, the meaning of the term "discrimination" in both cases was identical (Ibid, § 25), and the tests for determining discrimination were the same (Ibid, § 26). Although very brief, these explanations are extremely valuable in understanding the application of Article 1 of Protocol No. 12.

As in the previous case, the Court found it appropriate to consider the case under the provision of Article 46 of the ECHR. Again, it was stated that "the finding of a violation in the present case was the direct result of the failure of the authorities of the respondent State to introduce measures to ensure compliance with the judgment in Sejdić and Finci" (§ 37). Besides being a sign of disrespecting the Convention, this was also seen as "a threat to the future effectiveness of the Convention machinery" (§ 26), and "the speediest and most effective resolution of the situation in a manner which complies with the Convention's guarantees" was recommended. Specifically, the Court referred to the decision in case Greens and M. A. v. The United Kingdom (Applications nos. 60041/08 and 60054/08), where the Court questioned if it should provide the country with guidance "as to what is required for the proper execution of the present judgment" (ECtHR 2010, §112). As in the previous decision, the Court reiterated that the maintenance of the contested constitutional provisions was not justifiable eighteen years after the war (§ 40), and that every citizen of Bosnia and Herzegovina should have the right to stand for elections to the Presidency and the House of Peoples without discrimination.

Mr. Pilav complained that he could not stand as a candidate for the Presidency because of declaring affiliation with Bosniacs and living in Republika Srpska. In this case, the applicant only claimed his ineligibility to stand for the elections for Presidency and based his appeal on Article 1 of Protocol No. 12 to ECHR.

The Government contested the applicant's victim status as he declared an affiliation with the Bosniac people, and therefore the same restrictions were applied to the other two constitutional peoples. It was argued that simply by changing the place of residence, he could exercise the right in question. Because of this possibility, the applicant was not actually deprived of his rights.

The third case moderately differed from the previous two cases as the Court found that "the present applicant [was] theoretically eligible to stand for election to the Presidency", but "in reality, as long as he lives in the Republika Srpska he cannot use this right" (ECtHR 2016b). Discussing the case law concerning the residence requirement in the election process, the Court found that the residence mandate itself was not disproportionate or irreconcilable with the underlying purposes of the right to free elections, and that it could have a purpose in ascertaining the degree of the links existing between the individual applicant and the legislature of the country. However, the Court assessed that in the present case, the Presidency of Bosnia and Herzegovina was a political body of the state, with its decisions affecting all its citizens, no matter their residence. Because of this, the applicant could be concerned with the political activity of this body (Ibid, § 45). The Court found that the exclusion in this case was based on a combination of ethnic origin and place of residence and thus, this discriminatory treatment was a violation of Article 1 of Protocol No. 12.

In the case of Pudarić v. Bosnia and Herzegovina is remarkably similar to the Pilav case as both concern the ineligibility of persons declaring affiliation with the constituent peoples without residence in a certain part of BiH. The cases differ in the ethnic groups of which the applicants identify and BiH entity in which the applicants reside. The Court had already declared in its ruling in the Sejdić and Finci case that Article 1 of Protocol No. 12 was applicable in elections to the Presidency of BiH. Considering all the circumstances of the case, the Court found the applicant was discriminated against and therefore a victim of a violation of Article 1 of Protocol No. 12.

This ruling is important because it declares and confirms the provision of the Dayton Constitution concerning the elections to the Presidency BiH being discriminatory in other BiH entity as well. It will be interesting to see if there soon will be a case at the ECtHR concerning the discrimination of Croats from RS in elections to the Presidency and how this last decision would contribute to the execution of the Sejdić and Finci group.

Finally, the case of Baralija v. Bosnia and Herzegovina possesses some similarities with the previous cases concerning discrimination in enjoyment of the electoral rights in

Bosnia and Herzegovina. These similarities are reflected in the ways in which all the cases' applicants experienced violations of and discrimination in their electoral rights. The previous cases differ, however, in their dealings with the existing legal arrangements and the discrimination resulting from passive electoral rights. Meanwhile, in Baralija v. Bosnia and Herzegovina, the issue concerns a legal void "which has made it impossible for the applicant to exercise her voting rights and her right to stand in local elections for a prolonged period of time" (§55) as well as the election process' discrimination caused by the said legal void limiting a certain territory.

The Court ruled that "the State…failed to fulfil its positive obligations to adopt measures to hold democratic elections in Mostar", therefore, violating Article 1 of Protocol No. 12 to the Convention.

The Government argued that the applicant was not directly disenfranchised because of specific and individual measure or interference, thereby making the application *actio popularis*. Also, it was argued that the applicant did not exhaust domestic remedies. As a matter of fact, she did not use any local remedies but applied directly to the Court.

The Court did not accept any of the Government's objections. Although the classification of the applicant's appeal can be considered *actio popularis*, which is not envisaged by the ECHR for protection of the rights, this does not mean that the Court shall automatically reject it. The rights set out in the Convention or provisions of the national law cannot be declared in collision with the Convention rights or discrimination just because someone considers it so and is not directly affected by it. However, if a person claims that the law or the absence of legislation violates her/his rights and is a member of "class of people who risk being directly affected by the legislation" in the absence of an individual measure of implementation, the Court can accept such an application. In the case of Baralija v. Bosnia and Herzegovina, the Court considered that the applicant's membership in the political party and the presidency at the party's local branch were sufficient to consider her a potential candidate at the local elections, and therefore, "a member of a class of people who [was] directly affected by the situation complained of; she [could] therefore claim to be a victim of the alleged discrimination" (ECtHR 2019, §34).

Although the rule of the exhaustion of domestic legal remedies is prescribed in Article 35 of the ECHR, the Court rejected the Government's objection as the rule assumes that the domestic system provides an effective remedy in respect of the alleged breach. Furthermore, the Government claiming non-exhaustion of the remedy needs to prove that an effective remedy was available in theory and in practice in the relevant time; accessible and capable of providing redress in respect to the applicant's complaints; and offered a reasonable prospect of success (§36). In its case law, the Court previously ascertained that this rule must be applied with some degree of flexibility and without excessive formalism and that it is neither absolute nor capable of being applied automatically, as the circumstances of each individual case shall be taken into account. In that sense, the Court must consider the legal and political context of each country, as well as the personal circumstances of the applicant. Despite the Ms. Baralija's failure to use a constitutional appeal before lodging her application, the Court rejected the Government's objection, viewing it as ineffective given the whole situation.

2.3. The Impact of the European Court of Human Rights Decisions Concerning the Right to be Elected in Bosnia and Herzegovina

From the outset, it was clear that the implementation of the ECtHR's decisions concerning the electoral rights in BiH would not be a simple task. The preceding failed attempts at constitutional amendment are proof of the difficulty in achieving political consensus in BiH and the execution of the Sejdić and Finci ruling that clearly necessitated changes to the Dayton Constitution. The following decisions additionally emphasized the scope of the constitutional reforms. It is important to note that no BiH authority ever disputed either the Court's jurisdiction or the decisions' implementations. The country's general compliance rate with the ECtHR's decisions is estimated to be 42%, which is quite good compared to the total compliance rate of 48% (Hillebrecht 2014, 48).

The execution of judgements in Sejdić and Finci, Zornić, Pilav, Šlaku, and Pudarić cases have been assessed as the Sejdić and Finci group of cases. This is the Committee of Ministers' practice in applying for the supervision of cases that concern the same violation, or that link to the same systemic problem in the state, to execute them jointly. Because of its specific circumstances, the Baralija case was implemented separately.

The Sejdić and Finci group of cases is under enhanced supervision, which requires urgent individual measures, pilot judgments, and decisions revealing important structural and/or complex problems as identified by the Court and/or by the Committee of Ministers and interstate cases. The progress of the cases' executions under the enhanced supervision procedure are closely followed, and exchanges with the national authorities supporting the execution are facilitated. The ruling in the Baralija case is executed separately and will be examined later.

In academic discussions concerning constitutional reforms, it is widely accepted that the interventions would have to be minimal, as "a constitutional amendment [is] strictly limited to redressing electoral discrimination, in lieu of a larger package of constitutional reforms" (Milanovic 2010, 640). Even a minimal intervention in the constitutional text, would consequently mean changing at least twenty other important legal documents, including entity and cantonal constitutions (Kulenović, Hadžialić-Bubalo and Korajlić 2010, 4).

Some proposals regarding the implementation of the decisions in the Sejdić and Finci group suggested allocating additional seats for the group of Others in the House of Peoples and thereby omitting ethnicity as a condition for being a candidate for the Presidency of Bosnia and Herzegovina, but still keeping the same structure of one member from Republika Srpska and two from Federation of Bosnia and Herzegovina. Theoretically, everyone would have the right to be elected to the House of Peoples and to the Presidency but would further complicate an already complex decision-making mechanism in the country.

Bosnia and Herzegovina took some steps to execute the decision in the Sejdić and Finci case by submitting an action plan and updating it following other rulings in this group of cases. Already in February 2010, Bosnia and Herzegovina delivered a document prepared by the BiH Central Election Commission concerning the activities needed for the implementation of this case's ruling. This document put forth an ambitious plan of legislation changes that included the amendment of the state, entity and cantonal constitutions and Election Law in some two and half months that planned to amend the legislation, organize general elections in October, and implement the Sejdić and Finci ruling. The Working Group was established in accordance with the Action Plan of Council of Ministers of BiH for the Execution of the Sejdić and Finci ruling and the decision of the Council of Ministers of March 9, 2010 (Updated Information on Action plan, 2011). Proposals for the amendments of BiH Constitution by members of this Working Group (leading political parties—SDA, HDZ BiH, HDZ 1990, SBiH, SDS, SNSD) were outlined, and a report on its work was adopted by the Council of Ministers at a session held on December 14, 2010. However, no consensus was reached on adopting any of the proposed constitutional amendments and all the groups' activities ended.

The 2010 general elections in Bosnia and Herzegovina were held with discriminatory constitutional provisions still being enforced. Upon implementation of the election results, a new *ad hoc* joint commission of both houses of the Parliamentary Assembly was formed, with a task of proposing amendments to the Constitution of Bosnia and Herzegovina until November 30, 2011 and proposing a law on the amendments to the Election Law of Bosnia and Herzegovina until December 31, 2011. These proposals would be forwarded to the parliamentary procedure.

The Committee failed to reach a consensus on the constitutional amendments even after the deadline was extended until March 12, 2012 (Ministry for Human Rights and Refugees, 2012). Despite the representation of important political parties in the working group, no agreement was reached on the content of the constitutional amendments. In many respects, the group was doomed from the beginning, as each of the parties worked independently rather than together to submit their own separate instead of joint proposals of constitutional amendments to the parliamentary procedure.

In October 2013, the Council of Europe was about to adopt a resolution concerning sanctions to Bosnia and Herzegovina for the non-execution of the decision in the Sejdić and Finci case, including even the suspension of the country's membership in the organization. Due to the reaction and lobbying of the country's mission in Strasbourg, the minister in charge and the parliamentary delegation to the organization, it was decided to drop the potential suspension.

In the meantime, the ruling in case of Zornić v. Bosnia and Herzegovina was decided in 2014. At a meeting held on January 12, 2015, the Council of Ministers of Bosnia and Herzegovina adopted the Information on the finality of the Zornić v. BiH judgment and decided to task the Ministry of Justice with preparing an action plan that executed both judgments to be submitted to the Council of Ministers for adoption within 30 days. A prepared action plan envisioned two phases of the decisions' implementations: the first concerned the constitutional amendments, while the second focused on the amendment of electoral legislation. The first measure was to be implemented upon forming a working group consisting of three ministers from the Council of Ministers of Bosnia and Herzegovina—one member from each caucus of the House of Representatives of the Parliamentary Assembly of BiH, and one delegate from each ethnic caucus of the House of Peoples of the Parliamentary Assembly of BiH, as well as a representative of the Central Election

Commission of BiH. Once this group was formed (in the ten days after the Action Plan was to be adopted by the Council of Ministers), it was supposed to adopt its rules of procedure (within fifteen days), prepare a draft of amendments to the Constitution of Bosnia and Herzegovina (by the end of November 2015), and deliver it to the Council of Ministers to adopt and forward to the Parliamentary Assembly for further proceedings (by the end of December 2015). The drafted amendments to Election Law were to be prepared by the end of November 2015, so they could be adopted by the Council of Ministers one month after adopting amendments to the Constitution. A problem occurred, however, when other members of the working group were appointed — caucuses of the House of Representatives and one caucus of the House of Peoples, both of which submitted names of their representatives. However, two other caucuses of the House of Peoples did not appoint their representatives despite numerous calls by the Ministry of Justice, which caused the blockade in the judgment process.

Soon the Pilav decision also became final, eliciting the need for an updated action plan that would include this decision to the execution procedure as well. However, there has been no updated action plan on the execution of the decisions since March 2017 to the Committee of Ministers. According to this document, the updated action plan draft for the execution of the decisions was prepared, and a timeframe for its execution was reset, in order to be more realistic and achievable as the working group was not established yet (Committee of Ministers of Council of Europe, 2017). At the same time, in the House of Representatives of the Parliamentary Assembly, there was an initiative to prepare the draft of the constitutional amendments, which was then forwarded to the

Council of Ministers, who put the Ministry for Human Rights and Refugees and Ministry of Justice in charge of fulfilling the task. Since then, no significant progress in the constitution and amendments to the electoral legislation has been made, including the preparation of serious and professional proposals, apart from rhetorical discourses in the election campaign.

"The utmost importance of relaunching the reform work without further delay" (Committee of Ministers of Council of Europe 2019) was emphasized as the highest priority necessary to eradicate the current discriminations in the state's electoral system. Political leaders and all relevant authorities were urged to take all required actions "to ensure that the present continuing and long-standing violation of Bosnia and Herzegovina's obligations under the Convention, and in particular of Article 46, [was] brought to an end before the next elections in 2022" (Ibid). Certain project activities were noted as operating under the Human Rights Fund to prepare for the reform process. It was decided that in the next Committee of Ministers meeting in December 2019, a competent minister from Bosnia and Herzegovina should be invited again to report on "the progress made in developing and implementing the strategy necessary to ensure that constitutional and legislative arrangements are in place before October 2021 i.e., one year before the next elections" (Ibid).

Besides the Committee of Ministers, the Parliamentary Assembly of the Council of Europe as well as the EU and its institutions closely and regularly followed the process of these decisions' implementations. This issue was discussed at their meetings, with certain steps taken towards fostering the necessary phases of the implementation process.

Following the discussion of the Sejdić and Finci ruling at the Committee of Ministers meetings, three interim resolutions concerning this decision were issued in 2011, 2012 and 2013. These resolutions repeatedly emphasized the need for Constitutional and election legislation reform, the country's commitment to review its election legislation standards upon becoming a member of the Council of Europe, and the task of making necessary revisions. The revisions highlighted the necessity of guaranteeing all citizens the right to be elected and direct dependence on the country's EU integration prospects. The decision's execution further addressed other issues such as non-implementation of prepared action plans and the organization and implementation of holding elections according to the discriminative legislation. The authorities and political leaders of Bosnia and Herzegovina were called upon to take the needed measures to eliminate any discrimination in the election process, to prepare necessary amendments and to regularly inform the Committee of Ministers of achieved progress in constitutional and election legislation reform. Authorities decided to "examine the present case at each of its 'Human Rights' meetings until the political leaders and authorities of Bosnia and Herzegovina reached a consensus on the measures required for the execution of this judgment" (Council of Europe 2012). Leaders warned that "the legitimacy and the credibility of the country's future elected bodies" (Council of Europe 2013) could be questionable if elections were held without necessary reforms made.

The Committee of Ministers continued the implementation of the cases on its consequent meetings, held every six months. However, there was little progress made to be recorded at these meetings.

The Parliamentary Assembly of the Council of Europe also brought three resolutions regarding this group of cases. These resolutions additionally emphasized the continuous failure to reach the political consensus on constitutional reforms and the deadlock in the state institutions, as well as the worrying statements and possible actions of some politicians.

The Assembly stressed the need for reform of the overall challenging Dayton system (Parliamentary Assembly of Council of Europe, 2010), calling upon the Bosnian authorities to implement various improvements, including ending obstructionism and working constructively at the level of state institutions. This command aimed: to speedily enact legislation necessary to advance BiH on the path of Euro-Atlantic integration, to implement key reforms of the remaining commitments to the Council of Europe, and to establish a new, comprehensive local government.

The Assembly urged the country not to waste time on making its constitutional amendments and in appointing a member to the Venice Commission and other Council of Europe monitoring bodies. These resolutions showed the abyss the country was in. Overall, the country's progress since becoming a member of the Council of Europe has been minimal and remained in stagnation. Once again, the country was called to make constitutional reforms at the state and entity levels, based on the Venice Commission's recommendations (2012).

Resolutions reminded political leaders of the obligations and commitments they made on behalf of Bosnia and Herzegovina, prompting them to "shoulder their responsibilities, stop obstructionism and work constructively at the level of State institutions", especially on serious reforms and actions in areas of rule of law and human rights (Parliamentary Assembly of Council of Europe 2018).

However, the Committee of Ministers have still tolerated the non-implementation of their decisions and have extended the timeline. It remains to be seen if the next general elections in Bosnia and Herzegovina will meet the deadline for the implementation of the decisions.

The ruling in Baralija v. Bosnia and Herzegovina, like the case itself, is different from other rulings. Contrary to its practice of not determining the necessary measures for decisions' implementations, this time the Court did intervene and ruled on the necessary steps in the judgement. The Court did so because, on the one hand, the case resulted from a failure of the respondent State to implement the decision of the Constitutional Court and its ancillary orders, which could lead to situations incompatible with the principle of the rule of law. On the other hand, the situation requested urgent resolution as every citizen of Mostar who had the right to vote was a potential applicant for the next case, thereby creating a large number of potential applicants demanding an end to this impugned situation (Baralija v. Bosnia and Herzegovina, §62). The Court ordered Bosnia and Herzegovina to amend the Election Act 2001 within six months of the judgment becoming final and enabling the 2020 local elections in Mostar.

Shortly after the final judgment, major Bosniac and Croat political parties, SDA and HDZ, started negotiations concerning the decision's implementation. They reached and signed the agreement on June 17, 2020, in Mostar, witnessed by the OSCE Mission Chief, the EU Special Representative, USA Ambassador, UK Ambassador and High Representative. The agreement included necessary changes of the Election Act and Statute for the ECtHR decision's implementation, as well as the agreement on the amendments to the Election Act which would provide equal representation of the constituent peoples.

Because this opportunity enabled HDZ to gain the wanted promise for changes of the Election Act, prevented citizen inclusion in the process, and saw that the same parties that signed the agreement are the very ones that had been in power for the last ten years, skepticism around the achieved agreement developed. However, the international community representatives saw this agreement as an important step in the right direction.

According to the agreement, the number of councilors now reflected the population living in electoral areas, differing between two and seven. It was determined that no constituent people or Others could have more than fifteen councilors in city council. The amendments were adopted but later than planned, so the elections in Mostar were scheduled later than in other cities, thereby implementing the ruling in Baralija v. Bosnia and Herzegovina.

2.3.1. The Impacts of the European Court of Human Rights Decisions to the EU-Membership Process

The role of the European Union in Bosnia and Herzegovina has remained ambiguous. The EU in Bosnia and Herzegovina sometimes serves as a mediator between ethnic elites, a partner, or the one holding the carrot and the stick. Amongst the confusion of the roles, it is supposed to play, the EU in BiH has effectively done little.

Upon the decline of USA engagement in the region, it was assumed that the EU would play a greater role. This has not been the case, and instead, the EU has served more over the developments in the country. Perhaps this is in part due to the absence of clear criteria defining the EU's role. Bieber considers "the closest document to a list of EU conditions for state-building is the European Partnership Document" (Bieber 2011, 1793). The EU's state-building criteria includes police reform, cooperation with the ICTY, reform of public administration, the creation of a single economic space, and improvements in human rights protection, increased efficiency of Parliamentary Assembly, institutionalized coordination mechanisms between the state and the entities, changes to the constitution, and electoral system.

The overall situation in Bosnia and Herzegovina remains dire in terms of its aspirations to become an EU member country. Certain reform processes, which are part of the standard procedure countries go through on becoming an EU member, have remained slow in Bosnia and Herzegovina, with almost little or no progress for years. The country's internal organization, incompetence, and concentration of the most important competencies at the entity level, large administration, and many legislative levels are just a few of the factors hindering progress. Additionally, there is a non-existing political will for the implementation of reforms and high levels of corruption, combined with the constant political crisis among parties of the governing coalition. Furthermore, electoral legislation, public administration, and judicial system reforms, as well as economic development and the fight against corruption and organized crime are just some of the areas that need urgent reforms.

At the beginning of 2000s, state-building efforts were underway to assist the country with Euro-Atlantic integration. The establishment of certain state institutions, however, were regularly opposed by Serb politicians. Furthermore, the country's progress was imposed by the High Representative, who was aware of these actions' shortcomings, but had no other option except to foster progress in Bosnia and Herzegovina. Still, obstructions continue, and no single issue can be agreed upon smoothly without intervention and imposition.

The EU has significantly lowered its standards and conditions to help Bosnia and Herzegovina become a candidate for membership and to motivate its political leaders for reforms. Paradoxically, this has not produced any significant results, but instead has made the politicians even more reluctant to implement necessary reforms and tackle the country's serious issues. This has further harmed the EU's credibility in the country, which had already deteriorated in the war period.

Before the signing of the Stabilization and Association Agreement (SAA), many arguable issues in Bosnia and Herzegovina remained unaddressed, the Sejdić and Finci verdict representing one of the most serious ones. After the ECtHR ruled on this case, the EU insisted on its implementation as a pre-condition for the SAA to enter into force, cautioning that non-implementation would mean serious consequences for the country.

Apparently, the EU made serious efforts to assist the country on this issue through organizing numerous discussions, different institutions bodies' sessions and joint meetings to try to reach an agreement with Bosnian politicians on the measures to be taken until the 2010 elections, which otherwise would not be accepted as legal by the European Council or the European Commission. However, no agreement on the decisions' implementation was reached, primarily because the main political (nationalist) parties were not ready to give up what Dayton guaranteed to them. The elections went ahead, and the issue was simply put aside by the EU, although regularly mentioned in EC's progress reports on Bosnia and Herzegovina.

Four years later, the 2014 elections were held, and again no changes were made on the disputed rules for the election of members to the Presidency and delegates to the House of Peoples. The issue of the implementation of this decision became a political issue, and the EU was accused of unfairly and counterproductively conditioning the country's progress based on the status of candidates (ESI 2013).

In December 2014, a new EU strategy for Bosnia and Herzegovina was introduced, resulting in a joint British and German initiative, described as the last chance for the country. The country's leaders agreed to put the SAA into force and comply with reforms, including the implementation of the ECtHR's Sejdić and Finci decision. The primary focus, however, was on the much-needed economic reforms. Bosnian politicians were also requested to write a declaration of their commitment to the reform process, and it emphasized that no reform shall be imposed by the High Representative. Following this proposal, the SAA entered into force on June 1, 2015.

Bosnia and Herzegovina officially applied for EU membership in February 2016, after having been a potential candidate for years, without formally succeeding to submit their application. The country hardly managed to fulfil the preconditions (political, economic, and democratic measures) needed to start working on a Feasibility Study for the opening of negotiations on a Stabilization and Association Agreement in 2003. In September of the same year, the European Council invited the European Commission to submit its opinion on the merits of the country's application. In December, the Commissioner for the European Neighborhood Policy and Enlargement Negotiations handed over a comprehensive questionnaire concerning all EU accession criteria a country needs to prepare and to submit. The answers were submitted in February, but additional questions were asked. Collecting the consolidated answers lasted much longer than with other countries, and although country officials promised to submit the answers to the questionnaire by October 2018, they missed the deadline.

Finally, in February 2019 the answers were submitted to the President of the European Commission, but with twenty questions left unanswered. The explanation stated there was a lack "of comprehensive information" to answer the questions, one of which included the non-implementation of the thirteen decisions of the Constitutional Court of Bosnia and Herzegovina. Once those questions had been adequately answered, the Commission would give its opinion about the country's application.

In the interim report in 2018, it was apparent that the EU expected serious reforms from Bosnia and Herzegovina, including the amendment on the election law and the constitution (European Commission 2018). The following reports emphasized the same problems. One of them is the so-called Priebe's Report (2019), which attracted a lot of attention, especially because it clearly stressed the important problems in Bosnia and Herzegovina that had been neglected for years. The report is a result of the EU Commission's initiative for improving the rule of law in the country, which focuses on the causes of rule of law deficits and aims on improving the monitoring of the rule of law reforms and their implementation, as well as increasing the accountability of the legal system. The initiative includes the whole legal system, courts at all levels, prosecutor's offices, and law enforcement agencies, with a significant respect paid to judicial independence.

Rule of law is one of the fundamental values of the EU and a basic principle of the Constitution of BiH. At the same time, the inadequate respect for this basic principle of democratic countries has been often emphasized as one of the main obstacles in the country's successful accession process. Despite numerous initiatives and projects of many international and regional organizations in this area in the last two decades, BiH is still a long way from achieving the minimum criteria. The report aims to support the country in efficiently implementing the actions needed to make significant progress in rule of law enforcement. At the same time, the report is confined to a limited number of areas, particularly in the functioning of the judiciary system and in citizens' right to an independent, impartial, and accountable justice.

The Priebe Report once again highlighted well-known and old problems in Bosnia and Herzegovina. Although it mainly focuses on a limited number of rule of law issues, it inevitably mentions the constitutional and political situation in the country as the main reason for the stalemate. The institutional fragmentation and frequent disputes on the distribution of competences between levels of government, although indeed a problematic issue, also often "serve as only an excuse for not taking an action, a pretext to evade difficult debates for finding workable solutions, where necessary through pragmatic compromises" (Priebe Report, 2019). Additionally, the report emphasizes a high degree of dysfunction at all levels of public institutions across the country, further discussing how some key actors show no drive to address or overcome these issues through coordination and cooperation but instead do everything to obstruct any change that they consider not to be in their own interest.

The respect for human rights is another issue under question in BiH. The report states that the failure to comply with the ECtHR's rulings for more than ten years deprives BiH citizens of their rights and discriminates against them just because they do not belong to the "right group" or reside in the "wrong part" of the country (Priebe Report 2019, §29). These are fundamental democratic and human rights principles, as well as principles of the EU and Dayton Constitution. However, the report restates the non-existence of any serious action must urgently comply with ECtHR rulings; this is a serious risk for BiH to be criticized for obstructing rule of law principles and failing to promote the rule of law.

The lack of will from key political stakeholders to reform the judiciary is obvious. The judiciary in BiH requires systemic reforms that are in the interest of the country and its citizens as they are crucial to improving the overall economic situation in the country. But the reforms are impossible without political and institutional will and have to be based on an inclusive, transparent process, independent of the party, ethnic or entity divisions and must presuppose commitment, ownership, and engagement of the whole society. Unfortunately, it is questionable when, if ever, this will be achieved in BiH.

The institutions in BiH lack a culture of responsibility, accountability and transparency, and the laws and their application in practice are in discord. This is reflected in the execution of the laws, and the existing gap between legislation and practice is worrying. Although most of the adopted laws are in harmony with European standards, their positivist and formalist implementation and frequent deliberate misinterpretation disables or makes difficult law's correct and meaningful application.

The other important problem is in the work, professionalism and impartiality in the operations of the High Judicial and Prosecutorial Council, which are indicated in this report. The problem of alleged corruption of its president additionally weakens already destroyed citizens' confidence in the judiciary. This body as well as the procedure for its election and disciplinary procedures must be reformed urgently. Appointment and promotion of judges based on ethnic principles is not an advantage in this sense as the training quality and duration for newly appointed judges and prosecutors is also in need of reform. Furthermore, both civil and criminal proceedings last too long and are thus cumbersome and inefficient. Cooperation between prosecutors and police is on an exceptionally low level with no coordination between their work. Even the Ombudsman institution is politicized and lacks independence. The existing problems with the prosecution of war crimes only add to the problems in rule of law in BiH.

The Priebe Report points to the necessity of constitutional reform in BiH as well. The report describes the issue and the available mechanisms for reform as "a question of political will" and "interpretative courage". Namely, the transfer of competencies from entity level to state level is such a mechanism. At the same time, no country could be functional with so many levels of government and what the report calls "institutional overkill", meaning fourteen different legal jurisdictions in a state as small as BiH.

On the one hand, the main shortcoming of this report is the lack of concrete recommendations for action or reform steps. For comparison, similar reports prepared earlier by the same experts for other Western Balkan countries contained the exact list of recommendations. Of course, specific constitutional situations and characteristic problems contribute to the complexity of the problem and make it harder to make any concrete recommendations which could be implemented independently of these issues. On the other hand, the significance of this report is exceptional. It is the first time that the complete constitutional and legal situation in BiH was analyzed in detail, with all important problems in the rule of law areas listed in one report.

One of the most important obstacles in the process of EU integration is the fact that a "significant number of the competencies relevant to the process of European integration, is the responsibility of the entities as well as the cantons" (Begić 2016, 12), and there is not enough coordination between the state and the entity level, nor the Federation and canton levels in exercising these competencies. Consequently, the implementation of the commitments deriving from the EU integration process, and those from other international agreements, is constantly blocked. To make progress, Bosnia and Herzegovina will inevitably have to go through a series of serious constitutional changes. However, currently there is no political will for this step. Political elites fail to reach an agreement on the common state, its vision and future, while major international actors are reluctant to decide and actively work on the future of the Bosnian state to determine the best way forward (Keil and Kudlenko 2015, 482). Important questions for the country's future are left to be decided by "a handful of politicians together with technocrats, without broader public engagement or awareness" (Perry 2015, 14).

The sad reality is that there is only a sole declarative commitment of Bosnia and Herzegovina's government for the execution of the ECtHR decisions concerning the electoral rights in BiH. Whether this inaction will continue to be tolerated remains to be seen. Some argue that the Council of Europe and the European Union should be "more forceful" regarding the implementation of the Sejdić and Finci group of decisions, because non-implementation puts both the European Court's Protocol 12 jurisprudence and the European anti-discrimination standards generally at risk (Raulston 2018, 703). This would make Bosnia and Herzegovina "take its ties to the European community and requirements for EU accession seriously" (Ibid).

3. Protection of the Right to be Elected in the Americas and Africa

The first part of this book analyzed the theoretical and conceptual development of the right to be elected as a human right. It examined the relevant provisions of the regional human rights documents and indicated the guarantees for the protection of this right within these legal documents. Like the European human rights regime, American and African human rights regimes guarantee the protection of the right to be elected, and both the American Convention and the African Charter contain relevant provisions with these guarantees. As explained in the first part of this book, the provisions and the rights guaranteed differ, impacting regional human rights regimes' courts' case law.

This part of the book will analyze the case law of the Inter-American Court of Human Rights (IACtHR) and the African Court for Human and Peoples Rights (ACtHPR) concerning the relevant provisions for the protection of the right to be elected.

3.1. Inter-American Court of Human Rights Case Law

The American Convention was adopted after the Inter-American Specialized Conference on Human Rights, on November 22, 1969, in the city of San José, Costa Rica. It entered into force on July 18, 1978, pursuant to Article 74(2) of the Convention. The IACtHR started working in June 1979, when it held its first hearing in Washington D.C. to move its headquarters to San José, Costa Rica the following year upon the invitation of the Costa Rican government. This completed the American human rights regime, enabling the tribunal to start creating its case law.

The IACtHR is known for its advisory jurisdiction, which broader than the one of ECtHR, and applied not only to the rights guaranteed by the ACHR but also to other human rights documents and other contentious cases where it has found a violation (Neuman 2008, 102). In its twenty-seven advisory opinions, the IACtHR dealt with different legal issues including the instruments of international protection of human rights, freedom of expression, restrictions to the death penalty and ACHR, judicial guarantees in states of emergency, rights of children, rights of undocumented migrants, the environment and human rights, gender identity, equality, and non-discrimination regarding same-sex couples (IACtHR, 2021).

Through the advisory opinions and its rulings, the IACtHR significantly contributed to the development of human rights protection and the establishment of international public order in the Americas. Its interpretation of the ACHR has been evolutive, considering that the ACHR is a living instrument (Trindade 2009, 24). This way, the IACtHR "has set limits to State voluntarism, has safeguarded the integrity of the American Convention and the primacy of considerations of *ordre public* over the will of individual States, has set higher standards of State behavior and established some degree of control over the interposition of undue restrictions by States, and has reassuringly enhanced the position of individuals as subjects of the International Law of Human Rights, with full procedural capacity" (Ibid, 25). However, the most important challenge in the IACtHR's work is the "lack of adequate human and financial resources" (Goldman 2009, 882).

When analyzing the human rights protection in general and the protection of the right to be elected particularly in the Americas, it is essential to keep in mind that this regional human rights regime started its development only at the beginning of the eighties, and that the region had its own developments and dynamics that affected the priority in human rights protection. Post-transitional consolidation of the democratic systems was not an equally successful process in all region's representative democracies. Despite some important steps being taken, such as improving the electoral systems, respecting freedom of the press and the abandonment of political violence, the serious institutional deficiencies still existed (Abramovich 2009, 9).

In this period, the protection of political rights, naturally, was falling behind the protection of fundamental rights. Initially, at the beginning of the 1980s, the IACtHR mainly issued its advisory opinions on fundamental issues of democracy and human rights to contribute with its jurisprudence over the decade to the political opening in Latin America, especially through helping to articulate the responsibilities of the states in guaranteeing the rights of its citizens. In 1991 all Latin American countries, except Cuba, had elected democratic governments for the first time in history. Therefore, in the 1980s the human rights regime development was merely "the result of the interaction of internal change and normative external concern about the conditions of human rights in key regional states" (Serrano 2010, 17), while in the 1990s it became "an integral part of regional politics" (Ibid).

Of course, the effective protection of human rights depended and will always depend on individual states and their commitment to democratic principles. That is also the case with the protection of the electoral rights in the

Americas. And though the democratization in the region expanded in the last decades, that process was not always followed with improvements in human rights protection.

The provision of Article 23 of ACHR is more detailed in regulating the electoral rights than the corresponding provisions of the other two regional human rights documents — while the provisions of both AfCHPR and ECHR do not directly guarantee the right to vote and to be elected, the ACHR does guarantee them in Article 23(1)b. The provision also guarantees political participation in line 1a and access to the public service of the country in line 1c. The second line of the provision is particularly important as it limits the reasons that can justify limitation or exclusion of guaranteed rights. These reasons are age, nationality, residence, language, education, civil and mental capacity, or sentencing by a competent court in criminal proceedings.

The IACtHR found violations of Article 23 in twelve cases, out of which seven cases concerned the violation of Article 23(1): Article 23(1)a was violated in case of Carpio Nicolle et al. v. Guatemala (2004), Article 23(1)b in cases Carpio Nicolle et al. v. Guatemala (2004), and López Mendoza v. Venezuela (2011), and Article 23(1)c in Constitutional Court v. Peru (2001), Carpio Nicolle et al. v. Guatemala (2004), Reverón Trujillo v. Venezuela (2009), Constitutional Tribunal (Camba Campos et al.) v. Ecuador (2013), López Lone et al. v. Honduras (2015).

Two of these cases are most important for the analysis. Those are the case of Carpio Nicolle et al. v. Guatemala (2004) and the case of López Mendoza v. Venezuela (2011). The first case has roots in the 1980s, when paramilitary groups, known as the Civilian Self-Defense Patrols, emerged under the influence of the state army. These forces formed to organize civilian populations against the guerrilla movement, and they carried out many activities for the army, which included executions and arbitrary kidnappings. Civilian Self-Defense Patrols received resources, arms, training, and direct orders from the army and ambushed several politicians. One of the victims was a well-known journalist, politician and party leader, Jorge Carpio Nicolle, who had opposed President Serrano Elías' *coup d'état*. Nicolle and a few of his colleagues were killed on July 3, 1993, and the process for finding and convicting the perpetrators continued for almost a decade without any result. The Commission finally submitted the case to the IACtHR after the state failed to adopt its recommendations. In the second case, the applicant Mr. Leopoldo López Mendoza was an executive in the State's main oil company and former major of the municipality of Chacao but opposed the government and was thus prosecuted by the State Office of the Comptroller General for alleged irregularities in the transfer of funds, barring him from holding office from 2008 until 2014. The first alleged irregularity concerned the donation made while Mr. Mendoza was an executive in the oil company, and the second concerned the non-allocation of certain funds from the municipality to the district government. Mr. Mendoza unsuccessfully appealed to domestic instances, including the Constitutional Chamber of the Supreme Tribunal of Justice to finally file a petition with the Inter-American Commission in 2008.

In the case of Carpio Nicolle et al. v. Guatemala, both the commission and the Court found many convention rights violations from the victims and their detriments, consequently. Those rights are: Article 4(1) — prohibition of arbitrary deprivation of life, Article 5(1) — the right to physical, mental, and moral integrity, Article 5(2) — prohibition of torture, and cruel, inhumane or degrading treatment, Article 19 – rights of the child, Article 13(1) – the right to seek, receive, and impart information and ideas, 13(2)(a) – prohibition of a priori censorship, and 13(3) – prohibition of restriction of freedom of expression by indirect means, Article 8(1) – the right to a hearing within reasonable time by a competent and independent tribunal, Article 25 – the right to judicial protection, and Article 23(1)(a) – the right to participate in public affairs, (b) – the right to elect and be elected, and (c) – the right to have access to public service. The violation of the right to elect and be elected was found in case of the detriments of Mr. Nicolle, but the Court did not make any additional clarifications in this context.

In López Mendoza v. Venezuela (2011), the Court found a violation of Mr. López Mendoza's right to elect and be elected, the right to recourse before a competent tribunal, and the right to a hearing within a reasonable time. The Commission found violation of Article 8(1) – the right to a hearing within reasonable time by a competent and independent tribunal, Article 23 – the right to participate in government, Article 25 – the right to judicial protection, all in relation to: Article 1(1) – obligation to respect rights, Article 2 – obligation to give domestic legal effect to rights of the American Convention and submitted the case to the Court upon state's failure to adopt its recommendations. Additionally, the applicant complained about the violation of Article 24 – the right to equal protection of the American Convention. The Court found unanimously that Venezuela had violated Article 23(1)(b), and Article 23(2) in relation to Article 1(1) of the Convention.

In this ruling, the Court explained that the right contained in Article 23(1) – right to elect and be elected – implies the opportunity to exercise that right, meaning that the states have "the obligation to guarantee with positive measures that anyone who holds formal political rights has a real opportunity to exercise them" (§ 108). At the same time, the important issue emphasized by the Court concerns the restrictions in the enjoyment of the right to elect and be elected. While the Convention prescribes that the electoral rights can be limited only under the certain conditions, and one of them is "sentencing by a competent court in criminal proceedings", the Court found that this condition was not met in the current case — "the body that imposed the sanctions was not a "competent court," there was no "conviction," and the sanctions were not applied as a result of a "criminal proceeding"" (§ 107). Therefore, the sanction for disqualification of Mr. Mendoza from holding a public office unduly restricted and consequently violated his political rights. It is worth noting the concurring opinion of Judge Diego García-Sayán, who noted that other human rights conventions do not limit the exceptions to the restrictions of the enjoyment of the electoral rights to a criminal conviction. He also argued that limiting the suffrage is a serious infringement and that such deprivation is not proportional to the illegal act, as he instructs that deprivation should only be utilized to the extent necessary to protect against serious attacks on other fundamental rights.

In summary, it is evident that the American human rights regime provides a wider legal framework for the protection of the right to be elected compared to the other regional human rights regimes. Article 23 ACHR directly guarantees the right to be elected and prescribes the conditions in which it can be limited. This guarantee should lead to better protection and, eventually, to a better developed case law of

IACtHR in regard to this right. However, that is not the case—in fact, the IACtHR has ruled a violation of the right to be elected in two cases throughout its more than forty years of existence.

Additionally, it is noticeable that in the cases where the violation of the right to be elected is ruled, the Court also ruled the violation of the other fundamental rights—right to life, right to physical, mental, and moral integrity, prohibition of torture, and cruel, inhumane, or degrading treatment, rights of the child, right to a hearing within reasonable time by a competent and independent tribunal, and right to judicial protection. This leads to a conclusion that the right to be elected in the Americas is a protected subsidiary to the defense of the fundamental rights, and its protection is a concomitant type, resulting from the violation of these fundamental rights.

Beside the above-mentioned challenges concerning the lack of adequate human and financial resources, the main issues IACtHR faces in its functioning concern the rulings' implementations. ACHR does not contain precise rules but only establishes states' obligation to comply with IACtHR's judgments. There have been recently introduced reporting practices of the Commission and Court which aim to improve this area (Hillebrecht 2014, 44). With an estimated compliance rate of 34%, IACtHR evidently lags behind ECtHR, with countries' compliance rates ranging from 20% in Venezuela to 81% in Colombia (Ibid, 49). A certain freedom in this process is left to states, which causes some states' reluctance and slow enforcement of the rulings, with some even questioning the Court's authority in this matter (Abramovich, 23). Notably, the academic interest in researching IACtHR's jurisprudence in the region (Ibid, 25) and abroad recently sparked interest—there is little literature on the Court's jurisprudence available in English. In comparison to the European human rights regime, these are important obstacles to the efficiency of human rights' protection in general as well as in academic interest and research about the Court.

3.2. African Court on Human and Peoples' Rights Case Law

The African Charter on Human and Peoples' Rights (AfCHPR), which was adopted in 1981 and entered into force in 1988, envisaged only the African Commission on Human and Peoples' Rights as a body for the protection of the rights guaranteed in the Charter. This regional human rights document is specific in many ways, with the most important characteristic being its aim to reflect the African conception of human rights (Okere, 145).

The period in which the AfCHPR was adopted was characterized by an emerging and ongoing democratization process on the continent, so for many states, ensuring the respect of basic human rights was a challenge. Since then, the continent registered significant development in the protection of human rights, and the norms and the institutions for human rights protection and promotion emerged (Juma 2007, 1). However, even today Africa is the continent with a variety of existing systems, ranging from developed democracies to authoritarian regimes (Daly and Wiebusch 2018, 296). Consequently, the African states are facing various challenges including "systematic violations of human rights, relating to ongoing conflict, humanitarian crises, internal displacement of peoples, terrorist attacks, political instability, widespread use of torture and ill-treatment by law-enforcement and security forces, arbitrary arrest and detention, abduction and killing of human rights defenders and political opponents, restrictions on freedom of expression and limitations on access to information" (Ibid).

The idea of establishing the regional human rights court in Africa had been present since 1961, when it was discussed at the conference of African jurists. The need for a regional human rights tribunal on the continent became apparent with time, and the African Court on Human and Peoples' Rights (ACtHPR) was established by the 1998 Protocol to the AfCHPR as a way to complement the protective work of the African Commission. The Protocol entered into force in 2004, and the Court issued its first interim judgment in 2009. A full merits judgment was not issued until 2013, and until now the number of total issued merits judgments is twenty-seven (ACtHPR, 2021).

However, the various forms of resistance from key civil society actors like national governments, national courts, and NGOs to the Court are evident (Daly and Wiebusch 2018, 300). The most salient is the resistance by national governments reflected in the ratification of Protocol to the AfCHPR—out of fifty-five states belonging to the African Union (AU), only thirty-one ratified the Court's founding Protocol, and currently, only six countries made special declaration that allows petitions by individuals and recognized NGOs (those with observer status before the ACHPR) to the Court (Ibid). The number of latter countries was higher, but recently Rwanda, Cote d'Ivoire and Tanzania withdrew their declarations concerning this mode of application to the Court (Ibid). These withdrawals were controversial and indicated the current mood concerning human rights protection in Africa. This situation is making the Court's work more difficult as the individual petitions are "the lifeblood of an effective institution and vital to an IC's development of a significant corpus of jurisprudence" (Daly and Wiebusch 2018, 301).

With both its advisory and contentious jurisdiction, the ACtHPR contributes greatly to human rights protections in Africa, however, many challenges remain. Besides the issue of individual application to the Court, the inadequate funding and the judges' competence also need to be addressed (Murray 2002, 195). The lack of financial and human capacities is reflected in the fact that except for the President, judges of the ACtHPR are engaged part-time, and the Court is funded by the AU and international donors such as EU, GIZ and others.

The Protocol envisaged that the ACtHPR would have the power to order reparations for human rights offenses committed in violation of the AfCHPR or any other human rights instrument conflicting parties would have ratified. This broad jurisdiction was criticized and feared, further described as causing disorder and the opposite result of the AfCHPR's goal (Rachovitsa 2019, 259).

The Court's rulings are binding but their enforcement is not guaranteed as there is no specific body to monitor the deliberation of the rulings. Instead, the Court submits an annual report on the State's non-compliance with its rulings to the Assembly, and the Council of Ministers of the AU (former Organization of African Unity—OAU) supervises the execution on behalf of the Assembly (Articles 29-30 of AfCHPR). This monitoring role is left vague and resembles the "naming and shaming" practice in the European human rights system—the consequences of continuing refusal to comply with a judgment are unclear as the Protocol only established the obligation of the Court to annually report on the noncompliant states to the Council of Ministers, without prescribing any precise sanctions for the states not complying with the ACtHPR's rulings (Martorana 2008, 603).

Among the decided ACtHPR's rulings, five concern the violation of Article 13(1) of the AfCHPR. This provision does not directly guarantee the right to vote and the right to be elected, but it does promise the right to political participation. The decided rulings concerned the problem of independence and impartiality of the electoral bodies in the respondent states (Actions Pour la Protection des Droits de l'Homme (APDH) v Côte d'Ivoire, App. No. 001/2014 and Kennedy Ghana and Others v. Rwanda, App. No. 017/2015), the affiliation with the political party as a condition for exercising the electoral rights (Tanganyika Law Society, Legal and Human Rights Centre and Reverend Christopher R. Mtikila v. Tanzania, App. No. 009/2011, 011/2011 and Houngue Eric Noudehouenou v. Republic of Benin, App. No. 003/2020) and deprivation of citizenship, and consequently the electoral rights as well (Kennedy Ghana and Others v. Rwanda, App. No. 017/2015).

The Court's first merits ruling (2013) concerned the ineligibility of independent candidates to run for presidential, parliamentary, or local elections in the United Republic of Tanzania (Tanganyika Law Society, Legal and Human Rights Centre and Reverend Christopher R. Mtikila v. Tanzania, App. No. 009/2011, 011/2011). In this ruling, the Court "unanimously found the ban on independent electoral candidacies in Tanzania's national Constitution to constitute a violation of the African Charter" (Daly and Wiebusch 2018, 304). Namely, in 1992 the National Assembly of the United Republic of Tanzania adopted the Eighth constitutional amendment, according to which only those who are members of and sponsored by the political party can be candidates at all levels of elections. This legal act was challenged by Reverend Christopher Mtikila at the High Court, which declared the amendment unconstitutional in its judgement in Civil Case No. 5 of 1993. However, the Government adopted another amendment which nullified the contesting of the Eighth amendment and consequently, the Court of Appeal reversed the decision of the High Court and declared the issue a political one, which mandated it to be resolved in the Parliament. The ACtHPR confirmed that the rights guaranteed in Article 13(1) of the AfCHPR are individual rights, and therefore the regulation of the enjoyment of these rights, as in the current case, derogates the rights guaranteed in the mentioned provision. The Court found that this was a violation of Article 13(1) of the AfCHPR and directed the Respondent state "to take constitutional, legislative and all other necessary measures within a reasonable time to remedy the violations found by the Court and to inform the Court about the measures taken".

In the case Kennedy Ghana and Others v. Rwanda, App. No. 017/2015, the applicants were Rwandan nationals living in South Africa, whose passports were invalidated, which they learned when one of them applied for a visa to the United States. The applicants were neither officially notified of the invalidation of their passports by the Respondent State nor given the opportunity to appeal the decision. They claimed that this was an arbitrary deprivation of nationality, rendering them stateless and violating some of their fundamental human rights, including participation in political life. The Court considered arbitrary revocation of the applicants' passports, which prevented them from returning to the Respondent State and consequently, severely restricted their right to freely participate in the government of their country, clearly violating Article 13(1). The Respondent State was ordered to reinstate the applicants' passports within three months of the date of notification of the judgment.

Finally, in the case of Houngue Eric Noudehouenou v. Republic of Benin (App. No. 003/2020), the applicant claimed that the Electoral Code from 2018 enabled only candidates of two political parties close to the government to run for elections and be elected to the National Assembly. This way, the elected legislative body promulgated, in secret, without national consensus, the Revised Constitution and the Electoral Code, which was later declared constitutional by the Constitutional Court. The applicant claimed that this amounted to the violation of Article 13(1) as well as the violation of numerous other human rights guarantees at the regional and global levels. The Respondent State argued that the right guaranteed in Article 13(1) of the AfCHPR must be exercised in accordance with national law, cannot be construed as a violation of human rights and is up for the persons concerned to meet the required standards. It was further argued that the state does not require its citizens to join a political party but to be registered with a political party before standing for elections. The Court confirmed the alleged violation and ordered "the Respondent State to take constitutional, legislative and other measures within one month and before the forthcoming election to end the violations established and to inform the Court on the measures taken in this regard" (ACtHPR, 2020).

Being the youngest regional human rights tribunal, ACtHPR expectedly bears a burden of a limited case law compared to the other two regional human rights courts. With a total of three rulings concerning the right to be elected, the

Court still manages to establish some standards in this area on the continent. The relevant rulings concern the eligibility for using passive electoral right and restrictions where the applicants are restricted to exercise this political right due to the affiliation with a political party or arbitrary cancellation of their citizenship. These rulings show that although not directly guaranteed in the AfCHPR, the right to be elected is guaranteed to every individual and protected by the ACtHPR while the restrictions in its exercise must be justified. Especially significant is the landmark decision in the case of Mtikila v. Tanzania, in which the Court unanimously found the legislative bans on independent candidacy in elections to constitute violations of freedom of association and the right to participate in public and governmental affairs. The Court found further violations in the non-discrimination provisions of the Charter, thereby producing a provision of the Tanzanian Constitution that was not in accordance with the African Charter. Although the Court ordered the state to take "constitutional, legislative and all other necessary measures within a reasonable time" (ACtHPR, 2013), the Tanzanian government refused to comply with the judgment or to report to the Court on any measures it had taken to implement the judgment (Daly and Wiebusch 2018, 306). This example clearly illustrates the situation concerning the enforcement of the ACtHPR's judgments. The Court ruled in the other two rulings, similarly to that of Mtikila v. Tanzania, that the right to be elected corroborated the importance of the individuals' unrestricted enjoyment of the right.

Like the IACtHR, the African court faces problems with inadequate funding and incompetent staff. The Protocol prescribes that the AU funds the Court's work and determines its expenses in consultations with the Court (Article 33

AfCHPR). This is often insufficient, so, except for the President, the ACtHPR judges work on a part-time basis, potentially affecting the quality of their work. The most striking challenge in this regional human rights system, however, is the characteristic resistance to the supranational judicial authority that continues today to exist following the establishment of the African human rights system. This resistance is reflected in the low number of AU member states, which ratified AfCHPR, and the even lower number of those which accepted declaration on individuals' and NGOs application to the Court. Currently, this number has decreased to only six states. This represents a serious threat to the whole system and could potentially cause its collapse. At the same time, this signals a guaranteed decrease in the ACtHPR's case law in the future. The resistance has another consequence: the states are highly hesitant in compliance with the Court's ruling, and some of the rulings haven't been enforced for more than a decade.

The analysis of American and African human rights regimes shows the similarities, differences, and specific characteristics of each of these regimes and their tribunals. The differences in the functioning of these regimes and their tribunals affect the protection of the right to be elected as well. The most important concern among them is the establishment of courts, jurisdiction issues, and the compliance rate with the courts' rulings. They further impact the courts' case law, rulings' enforcement and importance ascribed to each of the regional human rights tribunals.

The early establishment of the human rights tribunals, along with adopting the regional human rights documents, may have contributed to their better functioning. Both ECtHR and IACtHR were established along with the adopting of the regional human rights document, while ACtHPR was instituted much later after adopting the AfCHPR by the additional protocol, giving reason that this contributed to better functioning and acceptance of ECtHR and IACtHR but problems in the functioning and acceptance of the jurisdiction of ACHPR. Arguably, the inseparable existence of human rights norms and their judicial protection could have contributed to better respect for both human rights and the court itself.

The legal guarantees of the right to be elected contained in the ACHR and AfCHPR are both different from each other and from the relevant provision of ECHR. Hence, all these provisions guarantee the right to be elected directly or indirectly, through their interpretation. It is necessary to notice that the ACHR's provision is most detailed in regulating the protection of the right to be elected: besides directly guaranteeing this right, it also prescribes the cases in which the enjoyment of this right can be limited. This provision best reflects recommendations about the guarantees of the right to be elected from the book's second chapter. However, it seems that this detailed regulation did not significantly impact the case law: while the number of cases ruled in the Americas and Africa concerning the right to be elected is quite modest, the number of cases in Europe, where the legal guarantee of the right to be elected is narrower, is higher. This implies that, besides the guarantee of the right, other factors potentially affect the development of the court's case law, such as the regional trends and political culture. It is interesting that both IACtHR and ACHPR can decide about the violation of human rights guaranteed in other human rights documents, while ECtHR decides only about the violations of the human rights guaranteed in ECHR.

The difference between the regional human rights regimes is reflected in their case law and compliance with the rulings. Both the case law of American and African courts concerning the protection of the right to be elected is limited by the regions' characteristic problems and, as a result, the enjoyment of this right is restricted and violated due to (not) belonging to certain categories. A parallel could be drawn here with the cases analyzed in the second chapter, whereas the violations of the right to be elected in BiH also concerns the exclusion criteria—(not) belonging to certain ethnic groups. And although the exclusion criteria in America and Africa differs from the one in Europe, the right to be elected is in a way prone to setting these criteria as a basis for its restriction, no matter if in relation to fundamental rights or racial discrimination.

In summary, the comparative case law analysis of the regional human rights tribunals teaches that the right to be elected is progressively better protected in Europe, then in Americas, and Africa. And although this might be a modest progress, it is justified to claim that all three regional human rights tribunals significantly contribute to this. IACtHR sent a strong message for those who faced oppression in authoritarian regimes by asserting that their right to be elected is guaranteed and protected. ACHPR ruled out exclusivity of political parties and their candidates, clearly emphasizing the right of any individual to enjoy this right. Finally, ECtHR abolished the exclusive rights of groups in power-sharing arrangements. With Sejdić and Finci and the following decisions concerning the protection of the right to be elected in BiH, ECtHR not only set high standards for human rights protection and the protection of the right to be elected in

Europe, but also paved a road for other regional human rights courts to defend democracy and democratic standards.

Concluding Remarks

More than ten years have passed since the ECtHR delivered its ruling in the case of Sejdić and Finci v. Bosnia and Herzegovina. Since then, the Court has ruled five more times on the violation of electoral rights in Bosnia and Herzegovina and has persevered in its position that the Dayton Constitution contains discriminative provisions which unjustifiably disable some of its citizens' enjoyment of their electoral rights.

This and the following ECtHR rulings emphasized the discriminative nature of the constitutional provisions regulating the electoral rights in Bosnia and Herzegovina. Their importance both for BiH and for human rights protection development is immense. The ruling in the case of Sejdić and Finci v. Bosnia and Herzegovina was the first ever ECtHR decision where the violation of the Protocol No. 12 was declared. It further showed that the electoral rights, which are not in the scope of Article 3 of Protocol No. 1 ECHR, can be protected this way, in the case of discriminatory practices. Beside this, the decisions signify the importance in protecting the electoral rights of minorities and the supremacy of human rights and anti-discrimination law, even in power-sharing constitutional settings.

The substantial right at issue in these decisions is neglected in academic literature: the nature and protection of the right to be elected are not widely discussed, with only a few academic sources analyzing, albeit vaguely, the right to be elected and its protection on a national, regional, and global level. The right to be elected is a neglected right in theory and in constitutional law: only one third of the democratic countries' constitutions today contain guarantees of the right to be elected. The presence of this guarantee in the constitutions directly implies better protection: the rights guaranteed in the constitutions are less prone to amendments because it is much easier to change the legal text than the constitution. Of course, it is highly important that the constitutional provisions contain the guarantee providing the enjoyment of the right to everyone, with only exceptional restrictions, if any at all, and in accordance with regional and global human rights standards. The ACHR, for example, defines when and how the right to be elected can be restricted while other regional human rights documents do not contain detailed regulations limiting this right's enjoyment. The Global Citizen database shows that the restrictions concerning the enjoyment of the right to be elected in national legislatures differ depending on the election level (national or local) and type (legislative or referendum).

While the guarantees for the protection of the right to be elected in global and regional human rights documents differ with only guaranteed political participation or democracy in some documents (UDHR, ECHR and AfCHPR), others explicitly guarantee the right to vote and the right to be elected (ICCPR and ACHR). In cases where the right to be elected is not explicitly guaranteed, the additional documents from competent bodies of human rights regimes confirm that these guarantees protect the right to be elected as well, as seen in the example of the European human rights regime. Therefore, the right to be elected in general is a right which is recognized, accepted, and guaranteed in the human rights documents at the global and regional level.

The case law of the regional human rights tribunals shows that the right to be elected is not only an important political right in Europe but also in the Americas and Africa as well. Though modest in their number, the latter two regional human rights tribunals' rulings imply that the human rights protection of the electoral rights in these regions comes to the fore as well. The ECtHR has been developing its standards in this area for a period of more than two decades. It ruled on different aspects in the enjoyment of the right to be elected, including formal conditions of eligibility, disqualification due to prior conduct or affiliations, and disqualification based on ethnical origin. These rulings contributed to the interpretation of the provision of Article 3 of Protocol 1 ECHR and development of the protection of the right to be elected in Europe and globally, but also added to the discussion of the relation between power-sharing arrangements and human rights protection.

In rulings concerning disqualification based on ethnic origin, all the applicants are victims of the system established by Dayton Peace Agreement in its goal to end the 1992-1995 war in Bosnia and Herzegovina. The country's bogus postwar progress lasted only a short time, due to frequent impositions. Amending of the Dayton Constitution turned out to be crucial for the country's prosperity and development, but amendment proposals failed to reach the necessary political support in a country where ethnic elites' interests are the only legitimate and important concern. Following this, in 2009 the ECtHR declared that the exclusion of minorities—specifically, Jews and Roma people—from the elections for Presidency and House of Peoples in BiH Parliamentary Assembly amounted to discrimination. In 2014 the ineligibility of citizens to run for these positions without declaring affiliation with one of the constituent peoples was also declared discriminatory. Again in 2016 and 2020, another rule of the Dayton Constitution was declared discriminative by the

ECtHR—this rule prescribed that only certain constituent people's representatives could be elected from the territory of one entity, thereby, subjecting ineligibility to Bosniacs for the BiH Presidency if they resided in Republika Srpska and to Serbs for the BiH Presidency if they resided in the Federation of Bosnia and Herzegovina. It is yet to be declared in another ECtHR ruling that the Croats' ineligibility for BiH Presidency if residing in RS is also a discriminative rule of the Dayton Constitution. The final case decided at the ECtHR in 2019 concerned the ineligibility of citizens at the local level in Mostar to vote and to be elected because of the non-existing legal rules. This is the only implemented ECtHR ruling in this area that showed how local politicians can work together when their own interests are at stake.

The other two regional human rights tribunals—IACtHR and ACtHPR—are both significantly younger than the ECtHR and impacted by regional dynamics and specific problems in the Americas and Africa. Compared to ECtHR, their case law concerning the right to be elected is more modest. The IACtHR found violation of Article 23(1)b ACHR—the right to vote and be elected—twice (in 2004 and 2011), and ACtHPR ruled that the right to be elected had been violated three times (in 2013, 2019 and 2020) under the Article 13 AfCHPR—the right to political participation. From IACtHR's rulings, it is observable that the right to be elected in the Americas was violated along with and as a consequence of the violation of the other fundamental rights. In both cases, the initial issue is one of political nature—politically unfit individuals are disabled in enjoying their political rights. The African cases have a similar political background—individuals who were not affiliated with suitable political parties were ineligible to become candidates at the elections—only those who were members or were approved by certain political parties in Tanzania and Benin could become a candidate on a ballot list. Meanwhile, Rwanda's citizens not residing in the country were arbitrarily deprived of their passports and, therefore, the enjoyment of their electoral rights. AfCHPR ruled all these to be violations of Article 13(1) ACHPR.

These rulings showed that these two regional human rights courts also placed the same importance in protecting the right to be elected and ensuring the security of the democratic standards in these regions as well. In summary, all three regional human rights tribunals recognize the necessity of the protection of the right to be elected and accelerate their regions' democratic processes through the protection of this right. Compared to the other two regional courts, ECtHR's decisions are more detailed in their interpretations and set the standard in electoral rights' protection. In that sense, ECtHR's rulings clearly send a message that the right to be elected is an important political right and that the discrimination in its enjoyment is not acceptable, even when it is embedded in post-war power-sharing constitutional settings like those of Bosnia and Herzegovina. Although these cases are very specific, they indicate the important problems in human rights protection. Therefore, the issues ruled by the ECtHR are not only European but also global human rights problems concerning the protection of the political and electoral rights, the prohibition of discrimination, especially when it is based on ethnic origin (racial discrimination), and the relation between the power-sharing arrangements and human rights protection. The ECtHR's decisions will surely impact other regional human rights tribunals' rulings in the future because both IACtHR and ACtHPR refer to the ECtHR's rulings whenever they find its case law relevant to the cases they are deciding, as in the landmark ACtHPR's decision of Mtikila v. Tanzania.

Table 3 Comparative overview of the regional human rights protection of the right to be elected

	ECtHR	IACtHR	ACtHPR
Relevant provisions	Article 3 of Protocol No. 1 ECHR	Article 23(1)b of IACHR	Article 13 of AfCHPR
Relevant cases	Sejdić and Finci v. Bosnia and Herzegovina (2009) Zornić v. Bosnia and Herzegovina (2014) Pilav v. Bosnia and Herzegovina (2016) Šlaku v. Bosnia and Herzegovina (2016) Baralija v. Bosnia and Herzegovina (2019) Pudarić v. Bosnia and Herzegovina (2020)	Carpio Nicolle et al. v. Guatemala (2004) López Mendoza v. Venezuela (2011)	Mtikila v. Tanzania (2013) Kennedy Ghana and Others v. Rwanda (2019) Houngue Eric Noudehouenou v. Republic of Benin (2020)

Major issues	Racial (ethnic) discrimination in the enjoyment of the right to be elected in post-war power sharing system.	Violation of the right to elect and to be elected of detriments of the oppositionist politician killed in an ambush by state-sponsored paramilitary group; Restriction in the enjoyment of the right to be elected due to the conviction for alleged irregularities in the transfer of funds as an executive is the state's main oil company.	Ban on independent electoral candidacies (without an affiliation of political parties); Arbitrary deprivation of travelling documents and exclusion from the enjoyment of the right to be elected; Ability of exercising the right to be elected only if affiliated with one of two political parties close to the government.

The regional human rights tribunals are facing some challenges in their functioning, including lack of financial and human resources. The most common challenge for all regional human rights tribunals is one of the rulings' enforcement. And while this problem is present in all three regional human rights systems, its embedded causes and characteristic problems are different for each of them. ECtHR's decisions are generally well implemented: it has the highest compliance rate, and most states' compliance with its rulings is undisputable. Furthermore, the Court's jurisdiction is not questioned, and potential problems concern choosing the appropriate measures for the rulings' enforcement, which is generally left to states to decide. Meanwhile, the compliance with the courts' rulings in two other regional human rights systems is different: the compliance rate in the Americas is quite lower than in Europe, and the African human rights system faces serious issues with compliance in general and specifically with its competence for accepting the applications from individuals and NGOs. In the last few years, the already low number of states which accepted this AfCHPR's jurisdiction additionally decreased to only six states.

A slow implementation of the Sejdić and Finci group of decisions is merely an exceptional case in the European human rights regime. Like any other state member of the Council of Europe, Bosnia and Herzegovina never objected to its obligation in complying with ECtHR's rulings, hence, its politicians often expressed their willingness to contribute to their enforcement. Unfortunately, this seems to be only a declarative commitment as no important progress is evidenced. The ruling enforcement has been a major issue in the country in the last decade and has shaped the country's relations between ethnic elites as well as internationally, namely seen in the country's progress toward becoming an EU member state.

Beside the standard procedure under the Council of Europe and its relevant institutions concerning the ruling's enforcement, the EU additionally contributes to the ECtHR rulings' enforcement process. In that sense, the ECtHR rulings' enforcement was set to be a condition for BiH's progress in the EU accession process. However, it was decided after that this condition would be postponed for a later phase of the process. It could be argued that the EU's decision to postpone these decisions' implementation as a condition for the continuation of the EU accession process for BiH is not a good one. However, the EU has continued emphasizing these decisions' importance in its progress reports, just as the 2019 Priebe report clearly stated that the failure to implement the ECtHR decisions would significantly undermine the rule of law in BiH. This shows EU's commitment to fostering rule of law and human rights standards in BiH to aid the country in becoming a full EU member.

Despite all the issues concerning the rulings' enforcement, the importance of the lessons learned from ECtHR rulings should not be diminished. These lessons are significant because they establish and acknowledge future human rights protection trajectories. First of all, we see the emphasized importance of the right to be elected, evident in the Court's acknowledgment of the immense role the legislative bodies have in one country. While the provision of Article 3 of Protocol No. 1 ECHR does not directly guarantee the right to be elected but does the right to free elections, ECtHR interpreted this provision by guaranteeing the right to be elected to legislative bodies on the state level. These bodies are further responsible for creating the country's highest laws and even the constitution, therefore, it is essential that they represent all citizens. Nowadays, democracy is often equated with representation, and a system without this basic characteristic cannot be considered a (representative) democracy. Consequently, this means that the right to be elected and its guarantees tend to become an indicator of the true level of both the democracy and the democratization in one country. Second, a priority is given to anti-discrimination rules by the ECtHR. Although both the violation of the substantive right and the discrimination in its enjoyment were alleged in the applicants' claims, the Court ruled that there is discrimination in the applicants' enjoyment of the right to be elected, and thus, there is no need to examine the violation of the substantive right. The principle of non-discrimination has recently become the most important principle of international and human rights law, aiming to abolish any unjustified and different treatment of persons in same situations. Whenever one's inability to enjoy their right might be caused by different treatment, there is a potential of discriminative treatment. At the same time, in two of the analyzed rulings, the Court decided that there is discrimination for the same right's enjoyment based on two different anti-discrimination clauses of ECHR, and therefore, they interpreted the provision of Article 1 of Protocol No. 12 ECHR as a kind of a "qualified discrimination" for the cases in which states do not take any steps to correct the existing and ruled discrimination in their legislatures. This indicates the priority given to the prohibition of non-discrimination by the ECtHR. Finally, temporary nature of power-sharing arrangements is underlined, making the ECtHR decisions important messages to future peacemakers and creators of peace agreements. This attribute in itself is one of power-sharing's benefits in post-war societies' conflict resolution and peacebuilding, but it is also a necessity for their development and transformation into systems where human rights protection is a priority, without any compromise. ECtHR stated and reaffirmed in its rulings that power-sharing arrangements which guarantee exclusive rights to some groups are justified after the war, but not indefinitely. Once the state has shown its ability to take part in international relations, i.e., to become a full member of international organizations and regimes and accept its rights and duties emerging from this membership, it is also time to put an end to the exclusivity of power-sharing arrangements and treat all citizens equally, without discrimination. It is important to note that this Court's reasoning should not be understood as a devaluation of the importance of power-sharing arrangements and their role in conflict resolution. Power-sharing arrangements and human rights protection should not be opposed to or exclude each other. Rather, this relation should be redefined as the roles both power-sharing arrangements and human rights play after a conflicted period and in accordance with other important values and institutions.

Power-sharing arrangements have an important role in post-war and post-conflict societies. They are often the best available conflict resolution tool for bringing together opposing sides and bridging the period of negative peace in societies. These arrangements, however, have shortcomings. One particular downfall sees power-sharing arrangements commonly promote democracy even though they are not totally democratic themselves. The main idea of power-sharing is to ensure that certain groups are represented and are included in ruling coalitions. However, by securing this inclusiveness, other groups or individuals who are not represented are automatically excluded, leading to further human rights violations.

The mistakes from Bosnia and Herzegovina and from the Dayton Peace Agreement and the Dayton Constitution should not be repeated — no matter the importance of securing power-sharing arrangements in ethnically or religiously divided post-conflict societies. These arrangements must be established in accordance with human rights standards, including non-discrimination principles in the enjoyment of any guaranteed human right, or they should at least be limited to a certain time period. The non-existence of "sunset clauses" is one of the main shortcomings of the Dayton Peace Agreement and the system it established, which was never meant to last indefinitely. ECtHR clearly emphasized this attitude in its rulings when it was argued that the past conflict in BiH, although a very important factor for the country's constitutional setting and the overall situation in the country, was not sufficient in justifying constitutional discrimination in BiH more than two decades after the war ended and when the country already had evidenced some progress on its way to becoming a full-fledged democratic country.

Democracy is the alternative to authoritarian regimes and conflicted and divided states and societies. Hence, a state's opting for democracy is only the beginning of a long road in the democratization process. Even in established democracies, democratization can occur in a structure of reforms. Looking toward the future, democracy's importance shall increase, with elections and the right to be elected promising to be its most fundamental cornerstones.

Previous years and the continuing Covid-19 pandemic posed many challenges. The countries and their governments opted for various measures to protect the life and health of its citizens, and for this sake, other human rights were restricted all over the world. Political rights were no exception as they were among the rights at risk as well. According to the International Institute for Democracy and Electoral Assistance (IDEA), in the period between February 21, 2020, until December 27, 2020, at least 75 countries and territories across the globe decided to postpone national and subnational elections due to Covid-19. At the same time, at least 101 countries and territories decided to hold national or subnational elections, despite Covid-19 concerns. Furthermore, at least 49 countries and territories have since held elections that were initially postponed due to concerns related to Covid-19 (IDEA, 2020). This information shows that even during the pandemic most of the world's countries held elections, either postponed or on time, indicating the importance of elections and the enjoyment of electoral rights even in exceptional circumstances such as a global pandemic.

Elections and electoral rights' value will continue to grow in the future as well, and elections will remain the most crucial mode of citizens' political participation. Despite the problems concerning elections, like low turnout or electoral engineering to name a couple, elections may still provide the most appropriate way for citizens to impact the government and the decision-making processes in their countries. While the right to vote is almost universally guaranteed to citizens and even non-citizen residents, the right to be elected is nowadays restricted to many citizens in states all over the world.

Many important issues concerning the enjoyment of the right to be elected require further future research, primarily a theoretical framework which will provide justification for wider constitutional guarantees of the right to be elected to everyone without any restrictions. The problem of this right's conceptual vagueness however, remains. Future theoretical studies on this right should focus on clarifying the concept and its content. Only when the right to be elected is clearly defined will it be possible to advocate its wider guarantees in constitutions, without any or with minimal restrictions, allowing the possibility to consider it a positive human right.

A deeper analysis of the domestic legislature concerning the right to be elected is necessary. It would determine the content and conditions for the enjoyment of the right to be elected when guaranteed in national laws. This analysis would also provide important insights about the relation between constitutional guarantees and the conditions prescribed for the enjoyment of the right to be elected in national law.

On a final note, the right to be elected is a positive, political right guaranteed in the international and regional human rights documents and national constitutions and protected by regional human rights tribunals. However, not all national constitutions guarantee this right as such. To achieve that, it is necessary to emphasize and insist that the right to vote and the right to be elected are interdependent and coexistent rights, and that one without another cannot be fully enjoyed. Voters will fully enjoy active rights only when the enjoyment of the passive one is equally available. Once this aim is achieved in states all over the world, the right to be elected will become a universally accepted and guaranteed right.

Bibliography

— 2018. "Don't believe the Hype—Why Bosnian democracy will not end this October", available at: https://www.esiweb.org/pdf/ESI%20-%20Hype%20and%20Bosnian%20elections%20-%2030%20Jan%202018.pdf (last accessed on 19 January, 2019).

Abramovich, Viktor. 2009. "From massive violations to structural patterns: New Approaches and Classic Tensions in the Inter-American Human Rights System", *SUR – International Journal on Human Rights*, 6(11): 7-37.

Ademović, Nedim. n.d. "Opšti izbori u Bosni i Hercegovini 2018: pravni triler bez hepienda?", p. 8, available at: http://www.fcjp.ba/templates/ja_avian_ii_d/images/green/Nedim_Ademovic.pdf (last accessed on 10 February, 2019).

Arrighi, Jean Thomas, Bauböck, Rainer, Hutcheson, Derek, Ostling, Alina, Piccoli, Lorenzo. 2019. Conditions for Electoral Rights 2019, San Domenico di Fiesole: European University Institute.

Banović, Damir and Gavrić, Saša. 2010. "Ustavna reforma u Bosni i Hercegovini", *Politička misao*, 47(2): 159-180.

Bardutzky, Samo. 2010. "The Strasbourg Court on the Dayton Constitution Judgment in the case of Sejdić and Finci v. Bosnia and Herzegovina, 22 December 2009", *European Constitutional Law Review*, 6: 309–333.

Beckman, Ludvig. 2008. "Who Should Vote? Conceptualizing Universal Suffrage in Studies of Democracy", *Democratisation*, 15(1): 29-48, doi: 10.1080/13510340701768091.

Begić, Zlatan. 2016. "Legal Capacities of the Dayton Constitution in the Process of Accession of Bosnia and Herzegovina to European Union", *Journal of Politics and Law*, 9(1): 11-20.

Beitz, Charles. 2009. *The Idea of Human Rights*, Oxford: Oxford University Press.

Bell, Christine. 2006. "Peace Agreements: Their Nature and Legal Status", *The American Journal of International Law*, 100(2): 373-412

Bennett, Christopher. 2011. *Bosnia's Paralyzed Peace*, Oxford University Press: Oxford.

Besson, Samantha. 2012. "Evolutions in Non-Discrimination Law within the ECHR and the ESC Systems: "It TakesTwo to Tango in the Council of Europe"", *The American Journal of Comparative Law*, 60(1): 147-180.

Bieber, Florian. 2006. Post-War Bosnia—Ethnicity, Inequality and Public Sector Governance, Palgrave Macmillan UK: London.

Bieber, Florian.2011. "Building Impossible States? State-Building Strategies and EU Membership in the Western Balkans", *Europe-Asia Studies*, 63(10): 1783-1802.

Bojkov, Victor D. 2003. "Democracy in Bosnia and Herzegovina: Post-1995 Political System and its Functioning", *Southeast European Politics*, IV(1): 41-67.

Chandler, David. 2005. "From Dayton to Europe", *International Peacekeeping*, 12(3): 336—349, doi: 10.1080/13533310500074077.

Chandler, David. 2017. *Peacebuilding—The Twenty Years' Crisis, 1997-2017*, Palgrave-Macmillan: Cham, Switzerland.

Christiano, Thomas. 2011. "An Instrumental Argument for a Human Right to Democracy", *Philosophy and Public Affairs*, 39(2): 142-76.

Cirkovic, Elena. 2014. "Contested citizenship in Bosnia and Herzegovina" in Isin, Engin F. and Nyers, Peter. *Routledge Handbook of Global Citizenship Studies*, London and New York: Routledge, 455-465.

Claridge, Lucy. 2010. "Discrimination and political participation in Bosnia and Herzegovina Sejdic and Finci v. Bosnia and Herzegovina", *Minority Rights Group International Briefing*, 1-8

Cohen, Joshua. 2006. "Is There a Right to Democracy?" in C. Sypnowich, ed., *The Egalitarian Conscience*, Oxford: Oxford University Press, 226-48.

Dahl, Robert A. 2015. *On Democracy*, New Heaven & London: Yale University Press.

Daly, Tom Gerald and Wiebusch, Micha. 2018. "The African Court on Human and Peoples' Rights: mapping resistance against a young court", *International Journal of Law in Context*, 14(2): 294-313.

Dalton, Russell J. 2008. "Citizenship Norms and the Expansion of Political Participation", *Political Studies*, 56 (1): 76-98, doi: 10.1111/j.1467-9248.2007.00718.x

Diamond, Larry. 2003. "Can the Whole World Become Democratic? Democracy, Development, and International Policies", *CSD Working Papers*, 1-26.

Džankić, Jelena. 2015. "The Politics of Inclusion and Exclusion: Citizenship and Voting Rights in Bosnia and Herzegovina", *International Peacekeeping*, 22(5): 526-544.

Engelhart, Katie. n.d. "Bosnia's Three-Headed Beast: Sejdić and Finci v. Bosnia and Herzegovina and the case for "reasonable" discrimination", accessed October 1, 2020, http://production.sant.ox.ac.uk/sites/default/files/dahrendorf_k.engelhart.doc.

ESI. 2011. "Lost in the Bosnian labyrinth – Why the Sejdic-Finci case should not block an EU application", 1-14.

Fahner, Johannes Hendrik. 2017. "Revisiting the human right to democracy: a positivist analysis", *The International Journal of Human Rights*, (21)3: 321-341.

Fox, Stuart. 2014. "Is it Time to Update the Definition of Political Participation?", *Parliamentary Affairs*, (67)2: 495-504.

Franck, Thomas. 1992. "The emerging right to democratic governance", *American Journal of International Law*, (86)1: 46-91.

Gerards, Janneke. 2013. „The Discrimination Grounds of Article14 of the European Convention on Human Rights", *Human Rights Law Review*, 13(1): 99-124.

Griffin, James. 2008. *On Human Rights*, Oxford: Oxford University Press.

Harmsen, Robert. 2007. "The European Court of Human Rights as a 'Constitutional Court': Definitional Debates and the Dynamics of Reform", John Morison, Kieran McEvoy, Gordon Anthony (eds.), *Judges, Transition and Human Rights*, Oxford: Oxford University Press.

Hillebrecht, Courtney. 2014. Domestic Politics and International Human Rights Tribunals — The Problem of Compliance, New York: Cambridge University Press.

Huszka, Beáta. 2017. "The EU's Changing Conditionality on Anti-Discrimination in Bosnia and Herzegovina", *European Yearbook on Human Rights*, 237-250.

Johns, Alecia. 2014. "Conceptualising Political Candidacy as a Human Right", Ph.D. diss., University of Oxford.

Johns, Alecia. 2016. "The Case for Political Candidacy as a Fundamental Human Right", *Human Rights Law Review*, 16: 29-54.

Juma, Dan. 2007. "Access to the African Court on Human and Peoples' Rights: A Case of the Poacher turned Gamekeeper", *Essex Human Rights Review*, (4)2: 1-21.

Kartsonaki, Argyro. 2016. "Twenty Years After Dayton: Bosnia-Herzegovina (Still) Stable and Explosive", *Civil Wars*, 18(4): 488-516.

Keil, Soren. 2013. *Multinational Federalism in Bosnia and Herzegovina*, Ashgate Publications Limited: Surrey.

Keil, Soeren and Kudlenko, Anastasiia. 2015. "Bosnia and Herzegovina 20 Years after Dayton: Complexity Born of Paradoxes", *International Peacekeeping*, 22(5): 471-489.

Kulenović, Nedim, Hadžialić-Bubalo, Inja, Korajlić, Mirza. 2010. "Presuda Sejdić i Finci protiv Bosne i Hercegovine — Konkretne posljedice — prvi pregled", *Sveske za javno pravo*, 1(1-2): 18-36.

Lijphart, Arend. 1977. *Democracy in Plural Societies: A Comparative Explanation*, New Heaven: Yale University Press.

Lister, Michael and Pia, Emily. 2008. *Citizenship in Contemporary Europe*, Edinburgh: Edinburgh University Press.

Martorana Scanlon, Carolyn. 2008. "The New African Union: Will it Promote Enforcement of the Decisions of the African Court of Peoples and Human Righs?", *The George Washington International Law Review*, 40(2): 583-610.

McCrudden, Christopher and O'Leary, Brendan. 2013. *Courts and Consociations – Human Rights versus Power Sharing*, Oxford: Oxford University Press.

Merdzanovic, Adis. 2015. Democracy by Decree: Prospects and Limits of Imposed Consociational Democracy in Bosnia and Herzegovina, ibidem-Verlag: Stuttgart.

Milanovic, Marko. 2010. "Sejdić & Finci V. Bosnia and Herzegovina. App. Nos. 27996/06 & 34836/06", *The American Journal of International Law*, 104(4): 636-641.

Morawiec Mansfield, Anna. 2003. "Ethnic but Equal: The Quest for a New Democratic Order in Bosnia and Herzegovina", *Columbia Law Review*, 103(8): 2052-2093.

Morrison, Fred L. 1996. "The Constitution of Bosnia-Herzegovina", *Constitutional Commentary*, 13(2): 145-157.

Murray, Rachel. 2002. "A Comparison between the African and European Courts of Human Rights", *African Human Rights Law Journal*, 2(2): 195-222.

Okere, B. Obinna. 1984. "The Protection of Human Rights in Africa and the African Charter on Human and Peoples Rights: A Comparative Analysis with the European and American Systems", *Human Rights Quarterly*, 6(2): 141-159.

Pajić, Zoran. 1998. "A Critical Appraisal of Human Rights Provisions of the Dayton Constitution of Bosnia and Herzegovina", *Human Rights Quarterly*, 20(1): 125-138.

Perry, Valery. 2015. "Constitutional Reform Processes in Bosnia and Herzegovina: Top–Down Failure, Bottom–Up Potential, Continued Stalemate", in Soeren Keil and Valery Perry (eds), *Statebuilding and Democratization in Bosnia and Herzegovina*, Alderidge: Ashgate, 163–87.

Perry, Valery. 2015. "Constitutional Reform in Bosnia and Herzegovina: Does the Road to Confederation go through the EU?", *International Peacekeeping*, 22(5): 490-510.

Peter, Fabienne. 2013. "Human Right to Political Participation", *Journal of Ethics & Social Philosophy*, 7(1): 1-16.

Piscopo, Jennifer M. and Shames, Shauna L. 2020. *The Right to Be Elected – 100 Years since Suffrage*, Boston: Boston Review.

Rachovitsa, Adamantia. 2019. "On New 'Judicial Animals': The Curious Case of an African Court with Material Jurisdiction of a Global Scope", *Human Rights Law Review*, 19(2): 255–289.

Raulston, Elizabeth. 2018. "(Un)Justifiable?: A Comparison of Electoral Discrimination Jurisprudence at the European Court of Human Rights and the Constitutional Court of Bosnia and Herzegovina", *The American University International Law Review*, 28(2): 669-706.

Risse, Thomas. 2000. "Let's Argue!": Communicative Action in World Politics", *International Organization*, 54(1): 1-39.

Schneider, Cornelia. 2000. "The Constitutional Protection of Rights in Dworkin's and Habermas' Theories of Democracy", *UCL Jurisprudence Review*, 104-105.

Serrano, Mónica. 2010. "The human rights regime in the Americas: Theory and reality" in Serrano, Mónica and Popovski, Vesselin, *Human Rights Regimes in Americas*, Tokyo-New York-Paris: United Nations University Press, 1-28.

Steiner, Christian and Ademović, Nedim. 2010. *Constitution of Bosnia and Herzegovina – Commentary*. Sarajevo: Konrad Adenauer Stiftung e.V.

Tran, Celine. 2011. "Striking a Balance Between Human Rights and Peace and Stability: A Review of the European Court of Human Rights Decision Sejdić and Finci v. Bosnia and Herzegovina", *Human Rights Brief*, 18(2): 3-8.

Trindade, Antonio Augusto Cançado. 2003. "The Developing Case Law of Inter-American Court of Human Rights", *Human Rights Law Review*, 3(1): 1-25.

Van der Schyff, Gerhand. 2005. "The Concept of Democracy as an Element of the European Convention", *Comparative and International Law Journal of Southern Africa*, 38: 355-372.

Van Deth, Jan W. 2016. "What is Political Participation", Oxford Research Encyclopedia of Politics, doi: 10.1093/acrefore/978019 0228637.013.68

Wheatley, Stephen. 2012. "The construction of the constitutional essentials of democratic politics by the European Court of Human Rights following Sejdić and Finci" in Dickinson, Rob, Katselli, Elena *Examining Critical Perspectives on Human Rights*, Cambridge: Cambridge University Press, 153-174.

Decision of the Constitutional Court of Bosnia and Herzegovina, no.: U-5/04, from March 31, 2006.

Venice Commission's Opinion No. 862/ 2016, from 17 October 2016, Amicus Curiae Brief for the Constitutional Court of Bosnia and Herzegovina on the Mode of Election of Delegates to the House of Peoples of the Parliament of the Federation of Bosnia and Herzegovina, adopted by the Venice Commission at its 108th Plenary Session (Venice, 14-15 October 2016).

Decision of the Constitutional Court of Bosnia and Herzegovina, No.: U-23/14, from 1 December 2016.

Brief submitted by the High Representative concerning the request of the applicant in Case No. U 4/18, available at: http://www.ohr.int/?p=99294&print=pdf (last accessed on 13 February 2019).

European Commission-Commission Staff Working Document, Bosnia and Herzegovina 2018 Report, https://ec.europa.eu/neighbourhood-enlargement/sites/near/files/20180417-bosnia-and-herzegovina-report.pdf

Council of Europe, "Explanatory Report to the Protocol No. 12 to the Convention for the Protection of Human Rights and Fundamental Freedoms", available at: https://rm.coe.int/16800 cce48, (last accessed on 16 March 2019).

Council of Europe, "Guide on Article 3 of Protocol No. 1 to the European Convention on Human Rights — Right to free elections", available at: https://www.echr.coe.int/Documents/Guide_Art_3_Protocol_1_ENG.pdf (last accessed on 15 March 2019).

Case of Boškoski v. the Former Yugoslav Republic of Macedonia, Application no. 11676/04, from 2 September 2004.

Case of Mathieu-Mohin and Clerfayt v. Belgium, Application no. 9267/81, from 2 March 1987.

Case of Ždanoka v. Latvia, Application no. 58278/00, 16 March 2006.

Case of Podkolzina v. Latvia, Application no. 46726/99, from 9 April 2002.

Case of Sejdić and Finci v. Bosnia and Herzegovina, Application no. 27996/06 and 34836/06, from 22 December 2009.

Case of Šlaku v. Bosnia and Herzegovina, Application no. 56666/12, from 26 May 2016.

Case of Zornić v. Bosnia and Herzegovina, Application no. 3681/06, 15 July 2014.

Case of Pilav v. Bosnia and Herzegovina, Application no. 41939/07, from 9 June 2016.

Case of Baralija v. Bosnia and Herzegovina, Application no. 30100/18, from 29 October 2019.

Case of Pudarić v. Bosnia and Herzegovina, Application no. 55799/18, from 8 December 2020.

Case of Carpio Nicolle et al. v. Guatemala, from 22 November 2004.

Case López Mendoza v. Venezuela, from 1 September 2011.

Case of Tanganyika Law Society, Legal and Human Rights Centre and Reverend Christopher R. Mtikila v. Tanzania, App. No. 009/2011, 011/2011, from 14 June 2013.

Case of Actions Pour la Protection des Droits de l'Homme (APDH) v Côte d'Ivoire, App. No. 001/2014, from 18 November 2016.

Case of Kennedy Ghana and Others v. Rwanda, App. No. 017/2015, from

Case of XYZ v. Republic of Benin, App. No. 059/2019), from 27 November 2020.

Case of Houngue Eric Noudehouenou v. Republic of Benin, App. No. 003/2020, from 04 December 2020.

Interim Resolution CM/ResDH(2011)291 — Execution of the judgment of the European Court of Human Rights Sejdić and Finci against Bosnia and Herzegovina, adopted by the Committee of Ministers on 2 December 2011 at the 1128th meeting of the Ministers' Deputies.

Interim Resolution CM/ResDH(2012)233 — Execution of the judgment of the European Court of Human Rights Sejdić and Finci against Bosnia and Herzegovina, adopted by the Committee of Ministers on 6 December 2012 at the 1157th meeting of the Ministers' Deputies.

Interim Resolution CM/ResDH(2013)259 — Execution of the judgment of the European Court of Human Rights Sejdić and Finci against Bosnia and Herzegovina, adopted by the Committee of Ministers on 5 December 2013 at the 1186th meeting of the Ministers' Deputies.

Parliamentary Assembly of Council of Europe, Resolution 1701 (2010) — Functioning of democratic institutions in Bosnia and Herzegovina.

Parliamentary Assembly of Council of Europe, Resolution 1725 (2010) — Urgent need for constitutional reform in Bosnia and Herzegovina.

Parliamentary Assembly of Council of Europe, Resolution 1855 (2012) — The functioning of democratic institutions in Bosnia and Herzegovina.

Parliamentary Assembly of Council of Europe, Resolution 2201 (2018) — The honouring of obligations and commitments by Bosnia and Herzegovina.

Central Election Commission of Bosnia and Herzegovina, Proposal of Activities for Changes of the BiH Constitution and BiH Election Law aimed at Implementation of the Decision of the European Court of Human Rights in Strasbourg in case Sejdić-Finci.

Ministry for Human Rights and Refugees, Office of the Agent of the Council of Ministers before the European Court of Human Rights, Updated Information on Action Plan (No. 11-Ai-1/10-495/11), from 26 May 2011.

Ministry for Human Rights and Refugees, Office of the Agent of the Council of Ministers before the European Court of Human Rights, Updated Action Plan (No. 11-Ai-1/10-825/11).

Ministry for Human Rights and Refugees, Office of the Agent of the Council of Ministers before the European Court of Human Rights, Updated Action Plan (No. 11-Ai-1/10-37/12), from 20 January 2012.

Interview 20 with ambassador to Council of Europe Almir Šahović from 15 April 2015, available at: https://www.youtube.com/watch?v=0s0uhQuUtrs (last accessed on 28 April 2019).

Communication from the authorities (19/05/2015) concerning the case of Sejdić and Finci against Bosnia and Herzegovina (Application No. 27996/06).

Ministry for Human Rights and Refugees, Office of the Agent of the Council of Ministers before the European Court of Human Rights, Updated Action Plan (No. 11-Ai-1/10-755/16).

Committee of Ministers of Council of Europe, 1288th meeting (June 2017) (DH) — Action plan (14/03/2017) — Communication from Bosnia and Herzegovina concerning the case of SEJDIĆ AND FINCI v. Bosnia and Herzegovina (Application No. 27996/06).

Communication from a NGO (Minority Rights Group International), from 27.06.2016., in the case of Sejdić and Finci against Bosnia and Herzegovina (Application No. 27996/06) — Request for Initiation of Infringement Proceedings.

International Institute for Democracy and Elections (IDEA). 2021. Global overview of COVID-19: Impact on elections, available at: https://www.idea.int/news-media/multimedia-reports/global-overview-covid-19-impact-elections.

European Union Report on Bosnia and Herzegovina, 2019.

2019 Expert Report on Rule of Law issues in Bosnia and Herzegovina (Priebe Report).

ibidem.eu